'Having been in this situation before, this book really resonated with me. It helps to recognise the opportunity we have in front of us! But even if you haven't been fired, the techniques outlined in this book are perfect for anyone who wants to reinvent their life and start living the way they really want!'

KARLA CHAPMAN, Super Yacht manager and former 'FIRED' employee

'Stephanie's story is an inspiration to us all, and I thoroughly recommend this book to anyone looking for motivation to succeed.'

JAY GODDARD, PR Manager

'Having been fired myself, I wish I had had this book to read as I was processing the daily struggle of getting life back on track & the new job hunt underway. This book would have encouraged me, empathized with my situation and given me tools to keep moving forward.

Grab this book because its application goes beyond the struggle of being fired, it is that gentle, encouraging nudge out of bed that we need in those testing times when hiding under the covers is all you feel like doing.'

LIZ ALDER, Entrepreneur and former 'FIRED' employee

FIRED

FIRED

Why losing your job is the best thing
that can happen to you

STEPHANIE BROWN

Copyright 2017 Stephanie Brown. All rights reserved.

No part of this publication may be reproduced, stored in a retrieval system or transmitted in any form or by any means, electronic, mechanical, photocopying, recording or otherwise, without the prior permission of the copyright owner.

Every reasonable effort has been made by the publisher to trace the copyright holders of material in this book. Any errors or omissions should be notified in writing to the publisher, who will endeavour to rectify the situation for any reprints or further editions.

This book is a motivational book written to encourage readers to live the life they have always wanted. Any stories depicted in this book or real names of people or companies have been used as part of a personal memoir and none of the content of this book is a reflection on these people or companies.

Cover and typeset by Automatic Art
http://www.automaticart.com.au

In loving memory of Brooke La Pine

Your strength in the face of adversity is what gave me the courage to write this book. Your laughter and zest for life are what reminded me to enjoy the process.

CONTENTS

PREFACE	10
INTRODUCTION: WHY I'M QUALIFIED TO GIVE THIS ADVICE	12
PART I: AM I FIRED?	**25**
Chapter 1: Where is your Comfort Zone?	26
Chapter 2: You're in good company	36
Chapter 3: Fired with dignity	44
Chapter 4: Reframing your story	50
Chapter 5: You've gotta have a plan	60
PART II: PLANS	**69**
Chapter 6: P is for Passion	70
Chapter 7: L is for Loved Ones	80
Chapter 8: A is for Activity	88
Chapter 9: N is for Network	96
Chapter 10: S is for Soul	104
PART III: REBUILDING YOUR LIFE	**113**
Chapter 11: A new life with structure	114
Chapter 12: Rules for living	120
Chapter 13: Life after 'Fired'	128
Chapter 14: The sun will shine again	138
ACKNOWLEDGEMENTS	142
ABOUT THE AUTHOR	144
COACHING AND SPEAKING	146

PREFACE

In January 2014, I never could have imagined how amazing my life would be today. If I could have shown my 32-year-old self the transformation I'd experience over the course of a single year, the pain of the next chapter of my life would have been bearable.

I had just been fired for the second time in my career and I was unaware how excruciatingly tough the next seven months of my life would be. Nobody prepared me for the lows of unemployment - the disappointment when I missed out on jobs; the reluctant jealousy when I watched others achieving their dreams; the knocks to my confidence as I was rejected over and over again. It wasn't great heartache like losing a loved one, but it was definitely heartache nonetheless.

I was lucky to be surrounded by incredible family and friends who loved and supported me through this tough period. There will never be enough words to express my gratitude for their unwavering belief in me and my ability to recover from this setback.

The only thing that could have made this period of my life a little bit easier would have been if I'd known someone who had been through the same experience. Someone who could sit me down and tell me without any hesitation I would get through this. Not just because they believed in me, but because they had been there themselves and that they knew that far from being the great tragedy I thought it was, this period would define my life in the greatest possible way.

I had many doubts over these seven months. Many times I lay on my bed crying, questioning whether I would ever find my way back to where I wanted to be. Now, three years on, I can look back and realise that no experience has challenged or motivated me as powerfully as the experience of being fired. Being fired was in fact the best thing that could have happened to me.

I can't be there with you all to tell you what a great opportunity this is. I can't be there to tell you it's going to be ok. I can't be there to say that I've been there myself (twice!) But I can tell you that you will come back stronger and tougher. If I can't be there in person then writing this book is the next best thing.

My hope is that this book will help you to feel less alone. I want you to know that if you let it, being fired will be one of the greatest opportunities you have to create the life you really want. I want to kill the negative stigma that goes with losing your job and instead invite you to embrace the chance that life has thrown your way.

If you're experiencing the pain and heartache of losing your job, I hope that you find comfort in these words. But more than that, I hope that you feel uplifted and inspired by the stories and actions in this book to map out an amazing new life for yourself.

STEPHANIE BROWN

3rd December 2016
London, United Kingdom

INTRODUCTION: WHY I'M QUALIFIED TO GIVE THIS ADVICE

When you come out of the storm you won't be the same person that walked in. That's what this storm is all about.

Haruki Murakami, Kafta on the Shore

Ten years ago, on a beautiful sunny July morning, I came into work blissfully unaware that the bottom was about to fall out of my world.

My boss had arranged a one-to-one meeting for 11am, but as I approached the meeting room I noticed the head of our department was in the room as well. It was odd, but I was young and so naïve that it hadn't occurred to me what was about to happen. As I took my seat across the table from them both they launched straight into it with no attempt to soften the blow. 'Unfortunately we have to let you go', my boss said. I sat there in stunned silence - literally numb – before I burst into tears.

FIRED

That was the first time I was fired, but it wasn't the last. At the time of writing this book I am 34 years old and I have been in the workforce for 12 years. I've worked in marketing for my entire career and have enjoyed success in two of the world's most iconic global corporations. Twice I've been made redundant – taken aside and told my job no longer exists. I have also been fired twice, taken aside to be told 'we no longer want you'. I have also had the unfortunate experience of firing an employee I liked immensely but was not right for the role they were in. You could say I know a thing or two about being fired.

The first time I was fired I was just 24 years old. I had been living in London for almost a year having arrived from my native New Zealand 12 months earlier. For those who have not done it, arriving in London as a foreigner and without a job is a fairly character-building experience in itself. London can be a brutal place and no more so than for a foreigner looking for work.

After the initial anxiety of thinking I'd never find a job, I managed to secure a role working for a publishing company in South London. It wasn't perfect but I was barely out of university and didn't have a ton of experience to leverage, so dream jobs were harder to get. In reality, my expectations for working were fairly low at that stage; all I cared about was earning enough money for weekends travelling in Europe and Sunday pub sessions with friends. As it was I found I really enjoyed the job. They paid me well, it was interesting work and as it turned out I was good at it too.

Over the next 11 months I did well at work. Evidently my predecessors were not quite as capable, so it made everything I did seem so much more impressive. My boss loved me; the clients loved me; the team loved me. It was the perfect start to my London career.

Very quickly I found myself moving into my comfort zone. London was starting to become familiar to me, not just a wash of unknown buildings and unrecognisable suburbs. I had moved into a flat with my boyfriend - we'd been together just over a year and were young and very much in love. It was my first European summer and I was travelling every other weekend. I was making new friends, partying in exotic locations and generally having the time of my life. At that point in my life, I don't think things could have been any better, which is why being fired was such a shock.

My boss didn't pull any punches. Business had slowed so much so they needed to get rid of someone in the team. Despite my glowing track record with clients, they didn't feel I had a future with the company and so they were choosing to let me go. I would have hoped my boss would at least try to sugar-coat it, but no such luck. She was blunt and to the point.

I could feel my face start to redden as the emotional heat rose from my neck to my forehead. I felt weak and light-headed as I struggled to understand what was happening. My boss and her boss sat across from me staring as the deathly silence pierced the room. I had no idea what was meant to happen next. I was in complete foreign territory. So I did what every 24-year-old girl, half a world away from home, would do: I started sobbing uncontrollably.

In fact if I'd known then the uncomfortable effect a woman crying can have on a man, I might have cried even harder. The male head of our department was so visibly uncomfortable with the whole situation he looked like he would like to jump out the window just to escape my crying.

But this wasn't calculated revenge. The tears were real enough and I soon ran from the room in a state of distress. Too embarrassed to go back to my desk with mascara streaming down my face and risk having to tell people what had happened, I ran straight out of our building and across the road into the pub.

I remember that day as if it was only yesterday. I remember how beautiful the sunshine was. I remember how happy I had felt that morning as I prepared for work. I remember how good life had been. And I remember deeply the feeling of having the rug pulled out from under me. I was 24 years old, a lifetime overachiever, and suddenly I had failed.

HISTORY REPEATS ITSELF

Fast forward seven years. Since that painful day, I had managed to secure a position in a large global corporation and had loved every minute of my new job. By summer 2013, I was ready for a change and decided to take a risk on a new adventure with a small London brand that was about to be taken global. I left my big corporate job with very little hesitation. It was not that I was unhappy; it was just that I knew I had more to give and that I would not get there without a new challenge. In my heart I was sure this was the opportunity I had been searching for; I could not have been more wrong.

Looking back, I knew within a week that this small London brand was not the right place for me. The global expansion was moving at a slower pace than expected and the team, while nice enough, were so established in their roles that they weren't open to new thinking or ideas. In addition, my new boss – the entrepreneur who had bought the brand 18 months earlier – had sold me a job that simply did not exist.

For the next three months I was miserable. I knew in my heart it was not right, but I had committed to this job and I was going to make it work. Unfortunately, the problem with being miserable and hating your job is that it shows in the work you do. No matter how hard you try to make it work, people can see you aren't happy. It is very difficult to hide.

So when it got to the end of my three-month probationary period my boss unceremoniously fired me. We were in a café in central

London, discussing how I thought the first three months had gone and he simply said 'This isn't working for us. We're going to let you go'. It was the 13th December - twelve days before Christmas. I could not quite believe it had happened again.

Being fired for the second time was completely surreal. Unlike my 24-year-old self, at 31 years old I had much more at stake. This was not just a speed bump in the road, it was a massive crevasse, like the ones caused by earthquakes and I fell straight into it.

Still, I had been there before and hindsight would tell me there was a reason to be optimistic. I wasn't exactly embracing the 'opportunity' but there was a voice inside that kept telling me everything was going to be ok. I wish I had listened more to that voice. If I had, the whole experience would have been so much more bearable.

So why was it that this voice thought it knew best? What little nugget of wisdom had being fired for the first time produced in my subconscious? The voice knew best because history showed with absolutely no cause for debate, that being fired the first time was the best thing that had ever happened to me.

Life after being fired was in fact amazing. Not only did the experience force me out of my comfort zone, it turned me into a hustler. I had to hustle to find a new job. I had to hustle to rebuild my confidence and my career. It pushed me to places I didn't want to go – deep down to rock bottom – but then took me to places I had only dreamed of. Being fired the first time was a roller coaster, but in hindsight it was the best experience of my young life.

A PAINFUL START

After running tearfully out of the office that sunny morning in July 2006, I started on a four month journey that at times was excruciatingly painful. But ultimately those four months helped to shape an amazing new life. The experience of that morning laid the foundation for the next seven years. I didn't know it then, but I was about to find my first dream job.

At that time the economy was booming. People would say you could leave a job on Friday and have a new one on Monday. I would like to say it was that easy, but unfortunately it wasn't. My confidence had been shattered and I was in a state of shock. While I did manage to find a new job within four weeks, it was such a disaster it only compounded the impact of being fired.

The first job I found after being fired was working for a big London advertising agency. Their offices were immaculate and the location was perfect for post-work socialising. I worked with glamorous people in a glamorous industry, in one of the most vibrant cities in the world. It should have been the perfect role but it was not. I went from being happy and in my comfort zone to being an emotional wreck.

Looking back, it's clear that big London agency life was not for me. From the moment I started, I had a knot in the pit of my stomach that tightened every day. I have never hated a job so much in my life.

I was miserable. I would wake up in the morning and literally sob my way through getting ready for work; my boyfriend would have to coax me out of bed every day. On the 35-minute journey from Kilburn to Farringdon I would feel sick to my stomach; a feeling that increased with intensity the closer I got to work. When I arrived at Farringdon, I would prolong the walk from the tube to the office, sometimes going around the block two or three times just to delay having to face another day.

When I did finally go inside the building I would do everything I could to be invisible. All around me the office was buzzing but I felt completely out of my comfort zone. I offered nothing in the way of witty chat or funny stories. I sat at my desk in relative silence and would only really make conversation when someone spoke to me. I was that weird socially-awkward girl. Even I would have hated me.

The blow to my confidence from losing my job, combined with hating where I now found myself, made me depressed. Not the type of clinical depression that needs medication but definitely the situational type that leaves you weeping uncontrollably and unable to see through the bleakness of your day. I once read an article about depression where the author described the experience as your life becoming 'like a detached, meaningless fog where you cannot feel anything about anything, even the things you love'. That is what it felt like for me. I became completely detached from my life. Even my housemates gave up and stopped wanting to hang out with me. If it were not for my boyfriend I would have felt like I had lost everything.

Of course, I hadn't. I had hit rock bottom but in the grand scheme of life, I'd lost very little. I had none of the big financial pressures that many people have when losing their job. I had a wonderful boyfriend, friends and family plus I was healthy and living in London, one of the greatest cities in the world. So in reality things could have been much worse.

But the reaction to losing your job is never rational. Yes, better things are always around the corner but the blow to your confidence, as well as the disruption to your daily routine can be a tough combination and I did not take it well.

Hindsight is a wonderful thing. I look back on those four months and marvel at the incredible life lessons that were learnt in such a short space of time – life lessons that would serve me well the second time around:

- Nothing lasts forever.
- No one owes you a job.
- Life can change in an instant.
- Your reaction to the situation is what defines you.

These lessons have all stuck with me over the years. Lessons I was lucky enough to be absorb very early on in my life. Lessons that would serve me well not just in my career but also in the rest of my life and certainly the second time I was fired. If I hadn't learnt them in my early twenties, surviving being fired at 31 would have been much more of a struggle.

LOSING A JOB, FINDING A CAREER

Six weeks after I started, I quit my job at that big London agency. It all came to a head when I was trying to get a piece of artwork signed off for a large UK bank's sponsorship of the Premier League. It featured a Nike football so getting approval from Nike was the last thing to do. We were already late sending the artwork to print and when I finally spoke to the receptionist, she told me that there was a Michael Jordan event the night before and it was unlikely anyone would be in the office that morning.

I went to the bathroom and cried my eyes out; I had missed my deadline, my boss was furious and all because Michael Jordan was in town! This is bullsh*t, I thought. It should be me out with Michael Jordan, not sitting here crying in the bathroom. I walked out of that bathroom, marched across the office to my desk and wrote my resignation email.

Amazingly, one week later I got a call about a job at a 'big global sports brand'. They wouldn't disclose the name of the company over the phone, but I knew straight away who it was.

The following day I interviewed for a job at Nike. I remember sitting across from the woman who would later be my boss and thinking, 'Lady, I am not leaving this room without a job'. I had never wanted something so much. As luck would have it she hired me on the spot.

Starting my new job felt like someone had flipped a switch. I remember after my first week thinking to myself, 'this is where I'm meant to be. These are my people'. I just fitted in.

From the lows of those first days after being fired, to the highs of my first weeks at a renowned global brand, it was hard to believe that I'd come through the other end. But it was more than that: I had completely catapulted through about four stages of my career and ended up in my dream job, the kind of job you hope for but know it's probably out of your reach. The kind of job reserved for the inner circle of the city, not a youngster fresh off the plane from New Zealand.

I had come to London looking for success and ended up being fired from my first job within a year of arriving in the country. Four months later, I had the kind of job that the little girl from New Zealand had spent her whole life dreaming about. I was back!

THE SECOND BOUNCE-BACK

I will be the first to tell you that a cocktail of good luck and coincidence resulted in my job at Nike. Call it what you will – fate, destiny, God, whatever – but I know that this job, and the subsequent path it sent me on, was part of the plan the universe had set out for me. I worked at Nike for seven years and had some of the best experiences of my life, not just my career.

But all great things must come to an end. I decided in summer 2013 that it was time to leave my comfort zone and really start to see what I was made of – outside the security of a giant corporation. The opportunity I was given with the small London brand felt perfect but in hindsight, it was too good to be true.

Being fired the second time was equally tough and the timing could not have been worse. Losing my job 12 days before Christmas was about as challenging as it gets. It is also one of slowest times for the job market. Nobody is thinking about hiring and no one is leaving their jobs. There is nothing you can do but sit and wait. Added to which, being unemployed in London in January is a form of torture. Not only does the sun not rise until 8.30am, but a large number of Londoners engage in a crazy social phenomenon called Dry January (staying sober for the whole month). So here I was: unemployed and not knowing when I would ever work again, and everyone I knew was avoiding the pub. It was a killer.

January came and went. So did February. Every time I spoke to a recruiter they told me it was a slow time of year. So I reached out to everyone I knew. I had coffee with friends, friends of friends, recent colleagues, old colleagues, friends of colleagues. Anyone who would have a coffee with me, I'd lock them down. It did not matter if I thought they had a role for me, I just wanted to meet as many people as I could and hope that somehow the universe would connect the dots and find me a job!

Thankfully, by March I had managed to pick up some freelance work, which succeeded in easing the financial strain. I thought by then I would have a permanent job offer but no such luck; the job hunt remained fruitless. Whilst the good fortune of having a bit of money coming in definitely helped, mentally I was still in a downward spiral.

Everyone kept telling me I would have the pick of the jobs. 'You've got a great CV,' they'd say, 'you'll find a job easily'. Not so. In seven months of job-hunting, I did not turn down one job. Not a single offer came my way.

I went through rounds and rounds of interviews with different companies. I'd spend hours studying their brand, preparing presentations and researching their organisational structure. Then, after three rounds of interviews and 15 hours of work, I'd miss out on the job. It was heartbreaking.

March came and went. April came and went. May, June, July. It was mental and emotional torture. My confidence was in the gutter. Somehow, I'd gone from Brand Director to desperate job-seeker.

But I still persevered. Because I was full of hope and determination? No. Because I didn't have a choice. The alternative was to jump on a plane after ten years of living in the UK and move home to New Zealand. I did not want being fired to be the reason I left the UK. I was determined not to let that happen and so I just kept on pushing.

Finally in August 2014, almost a full year after I'd left Nike, I was offered not one, but two stellar jobs in the same week! It was an easy decision for me to make. Four weeks later I started my second dream job, working in marketing for one of Silicon Valley's biggest tech companies.

I had been fired twice and been through the pain of unemployment a second time, before landing another dream job. I was back - again!

WAS IT ALL SO BAD?

When I look back on both experiences of unemployment, it's hard to forget the tough times. There were more low moments than I care to remember but I view both situations in a completely different way than you might think. Instead of feeling anger, bitterness or resentment, I am grateful for being given the opportunity to experience both.

Tim Ferriss touched on this perfectly in his book 'The 4-Hour Work Week'. Ferriss, a successful entrepreneur and author, admits that he has 'quit three jobs and been fired from most of the rest.' Far from thinking that being fired is a great life-shattering event, Ferriss shares my sentiment that being fired is an amazing opportunity. Ferriss tells us, 'Getting fired, despite sometimes coming as a surprise and leaving you scrambling to recover, is often a godsend: someone else makes the decision for you, and it's impossible to sit in the wrong job for the rest of your life. Most people aren't lucky enough to get fired and die a slow spiritual death over 30-40 years of tolerating the mediocre.'

I love this last line. 'Most people aren't lucky enough to get fired'. I have been lucky enough to be fired twice. In my 20s, I definitely did not see it coming. Despite the initial shock and the pain of the subsequent job, it was a good reality check. In my 30s I did see it coming but the months of unemployment and job hunting was a character-building experience that could have only been replicated by an event more tragic. When I think about all the experiences I could have had that would have built the same level of resilience - divorce, death, disease – losing my job was definitely at the low end of the pain spectrum. Losing my job I learnt, was an opportunity to really see what I was made of without the deep heartache that comes with other such life-changing events.

It is easy to stay in a job we are good at and where life presents minimal challenges; it is not human nature to voluntarily create discomfort in our lives. So for many people the best option is to do nothing and to stay within the boundaries of what is comfortable.

One of the greatest gifts being fired gave me was the understanding that life is so much more wonderful when you push yourself beyond your comfort zone. I have been guilty many times in my life of holding back, of taking the easy road when I knew I had so much more to give. I often wonder how many more regrets I would have in my life had I not been fired twice and forced to create a new life outside my comfort zone.

Learning to sink or swim when I had nothing left to keep me afloat has played a crucial role in the successes of my life. I have succeeded not in spite of being fired, but because of it.

PART I: AM I FIRED?

CHAPTER 1:
WHERE IS YOUR COMFORT ZONE?

Every time you encounter something that forces you to 'handle it', your self-esteem is raised considerably. You learn to trust that you will survive, no matter what happens. And in this way your fears are diminished immeasurably.

Susan Jeffers, Feel the Fear and Do It Anyway

As human beings we are hard-wired to be constantly challenged; it is what keeps us knowing we are alive. Far from being painful and uncomfortable, pushing outside your comfort zone is in fact one of the most satisfying and rewarding experiences you can have. It can be awkward and difficult at first but you will struggle to find an experience that lifts your spirit as much as the experience of being scared of something, tackling it and then knowing you can do it.

Although some incredible people will voluntarily push their comfort zone every day, most of us are unwilling to put ourselves in challenging positions. We are more likely to avoid anything that is awkward or uncomfortable, to our detriment. I once read an article where the actress Charlize Theron said 'I don't think you can create anything interesting from a comfort zone. You have to work from a place of fear and failure.' This is the exact experience of being fired. You are forced into a place where fear and failure dominate and without realising it, you can start to create a life far more interesting than the one you started with.

The fear and failure were certainly present in the weeks and months after I was fired. I feared I would not find a job as great as the one I had just lost. I feared being fired would reflect badly on me for future employers and I feared I'd run out of money and be living on the street! I also felt like a massive failure as my inability to succeed in both roles showed huge shortcomings in my skill-set and capabilities. I reasoned with myself that if I couldn't succeed in these jobs, how would I ever succeed in anything else? I was off deep in the abyss outside my comfort zone. I couldn't possibly have been more afraid.

IT'S AS EASY AS LACING YOUR SHOES

So if being fired forces you out of your comfort zone, what does that actually mean? I have long been fascinated by the idea of this imaginary place in our minds that manifests itself physically by stopping us from doing things even when we know it would improve our lives. What I have always found interesting is that it is incredibly easy to increase the size of your comfort zone but at the same time, pushing the boundaries is the most difficult thing in the world.

Think about it: have you ever had a situation that you deeply feared? Maybe you really wanted to get fit but you were scared to go to the gym in case you didn't fit in. Perhaps there was a party you longed to go to but you were afraid to arrive on your own. Maybe a job you were tempted to apply for but you were scared you might get rejected? These fears tell you that these things are beyond the boundaries of your comfort zone.

You know that going to the gym will make you fitter, healthier and happier but your fear about fitting in keeps you away. You know you'll have a great time at the party but the fear of what people might think if you arrive alone keeps you at home. The job excites you and you think you'd be good at it but the fear of rejection means you don't apply. Because all three of these things sit outside your comfort zone, you continue to watch from the edge, wishing you could go there but not allowing yourself to step over the line. The barriers in your mind have physically kept you from leaving your home or submitting the application.

Then one day something clicks. Maybe you have a health scare or you're sick and tired of feeling unfit and you decide you not going to wait any more. You lace up your trainers and charge down to your local gym. Walking in the door initially is tough because your mind is telling you there is something to fear. But once you are in there you see people from all walks of life, all shapes and sizes, all fitness levels. You get given a program by a trainer, they show you how to use the equipment and you start to work out. Suddenly, the fear is gone. Your comfort zone has expanded and the gym now sits within it.

But the bit you find most amazing, is how incredibly easy it was to put on your shoes and go to the gym. The fear that had been holding you prisoner was in fact very easy to face.

This is also true for walking into that party or applying for your dream job. You don't need a unique set of skills or incredible talents to move beyond your comfort zone. It's the easiest thing in the world, yet the majority of us continue to restrict our lives to the bubble we create in our minds.

YOU NEVER STOP GROWING

As children we are constantly forced out of our comfort zone. From the day we are born, life is about challenge and learning. The basic challenges we face as a baby such as walking and talking become academic, sporting and cultural challenges when we reach school. Once we enter the workforce as teenagers we learn new skills or a trade. But as we get older, we decide that we are okay as we are. 'I am a fully-fledged adult now', we say, as if there is nothing more we can learn.

And this is where the majority of the world continues to live their lives: waking up every day and doing the same things they've always done, never expanding their comfort zone because fear keeps them trapped or ease makes them complacent.

I found myself doing this when I was 24. I had come to London at an early age because I wanted to find success in one of the biggest cities in the world; a city in my mind, where great dreams could be made reality. I left the safety of New Zealand to push my boundaries but during my first year in London I very quickly created a new comfort zone. London became easy and familiar. Instead of pushing into new places, I stayed still, enjoying the comfort of the little world I had created. In my heart I knew I was capable of more but my head kept me trapped. The day I was fired it all came crashing down. Suddenly the comfort was gone. The fear had returned and I had no choice but to face it.

What I discovered is that fear never really goes away. The focus of your fears changes as you face and conquer them but new fears appear in their place. Forced to face my fears the first time I was fired, I discovered the fear I would run out of money and be forced to live on the street was unfounded. So by the time I was fired for a second time, this was no longer something I worried about. But instead new fears crept in.

Of course I had expanded my comfort zone massively by that time but that's not how it works. There is always a new fear to face, or something else you can learn. Imagine you have faced not only your fear of going to the gym but you've dressed up and arrived at the party alone and applied for (and got!) that job you knew you could do. You have expanded your comfort zone to include the gym, the party and the new job, but still there are new experiences that you fear sitting outside your new comfort zone.

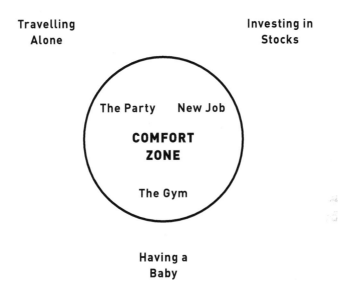

That's how the comfort zone works. You constantly need to expand it and there will always be new experiences to fear. Life is about facing fear; it reminds us we are alive.

If you really want to challenge yourself in a place outside your comfort zone, you need to be disruptive in your life. Disruption is caused when an event or series of events completely throws your life off course. All the bits of your life are thrown up in the air and you are forced to be patient and see where they will land when they come back down. Disruption can be voluntary or involuntary. Being fired is a form of disruption. Moving to a city where you know no one is a form of disruption. Quitting your job without knowing where you will go next is a form of disruption. Disruption starts off a chain of events that whilst not always being clear on where it will take you, will most definitely take you to a point outside your comfort zone. And that is where the magic happens. That is where your potential is fully realised.

SINK OR SWIM

The problem (or opportunity!) with being fired is that instead of pushing out your comfort zone little by little as most people do, you find yourself thrown from the safe place inside the bubble, not just to the immediate outside but miles and miles off into the distance.

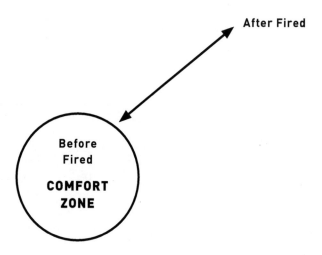

There are not many events in life – save for absolute tragedies such as death and illness – that have the ability to throw you so far off course. In an instant, you go from having a safe source of income and a strong sense of identity to drifting off somewhere in the abyss.

Being fired forces you to create a brand new comfort zone, and one much larger than the one you started with. The best part? You don't have a choice. You have to bridge the gap between your old comfort zone and your new one because there is no way back to where you were. We are forced to dig deep, to see what we are made of and to face life head-on in a way we probably haven't been forced to do in a long time. But however tragic and painful it may seem the experience has disrupted your world and has the potential to set you on a course to an amazing new life… if you let it.

REBUILDING THE LIFE YOU REALLY WANT

Think back to your younger self and try to remember the hopes and dreams that little person had. Are you living the life that little person imagined for you? For 95% of people the answer will be 'no'. Something happens to us as we morph into adults; we forget all the things we wanted from life and instead start living the life that is thrown at us. Life becomes reactive and we fail to *create* the life we want.

I am as guilty as anyone. Don't get me wrong; I've lived an amazing life. There is not much I can complain about. As well as enjoying a wonderful career, I've made two amazing relationships, travelled all over the world and had a lot of fun. But when I look back at what I had planned and what was thrown my way, the reactive side is stacked much higher.

Now I'm not saying that you shouldn't take the opportunities that come your way; you absolutely should! But only if they are taking you where you want to be. The only problem is, most people do not know where that is. They do not know the life they want to live or - worse still - are too scared or too lazy to go for the things they really want.

This is why being fired is such a great opportunity. One day you are chugging along inside your comfort zone. Next you are thrown outside it and the structure no longer exists. For all the anxiety and uncertainty it creates you ultimately find yourself with a blank canvas. You have the chance to re-evaluate your life and rebuild it from scratch.

Very few people are brave enough to cause this sort of disruption in their own lives; it goes against human nature to cause ourselves so much distress. But when it is thrust upon you, your survival instinct kicks in and you unearth strength and perseverance you never knew you had. The structure of the life you once had has been taken away and all you are left with is a unique opportunity to look at your life in a new light.

Both experiences of being fired achieved this for me. Once I realised many of the great fears I held for myself didn't happen or even better, they did happen but I lived to tell the tale, I realised that my perspective of the world had changed. I started to see new opportunities and possibilities that I had never seen before. While I would not go as far as to say I no longer fear failure, I often ask myself 'what's really the worst that can happen?' Most of the time I am surprised by the answer. There is a great comfort in understanding that most things we fear are actually not scary at all.

> **To receive the 'Week One Crash Course in Unemployment' visit www.LifeAfterFired.com to request a copy and find out exactly what it takes to own Week 1 of Unemployment like a boss!**

KEY LESSONS FROM CHAPTER 1:

- Our comfort zone is a place in our minds that keeps us from pushing forward with our lives and pursuing our dreams. When we are fired we are pushed out beyond the boundaries of our comfort zone and into a place where are forced to sink or swim. But this is also a place where 'the magic happens'.

- Expanding your comfort zone – through facing your fears – is often less scary than we think. But once we face our fear, our comfort zone expands and we discover new challenges to be faced. This is a good thing as it means we never stop learning.

CHAPTER 2:
YOU'RE IN GOOD COMPANY

A mere seven years after my graduation day, I had failed on an epic scale...I was jobless, a lone parent and as poor as it is possible to be in modern Britain without being homeless.

J.K. Rowling

When I was fired at 24, I was one of the only people I knew to have been fired. By the time I was 32, it felt like a club. At least five people within my close circle of friends had been fired from their job at some point. In fact, the second time I was fired my best friend in Australia was also let go from her new job within a week of me. It is much more commonplace than we would care to admit.

I know incredibly talented people who have been fired. I know incredibly smart people who have been fired. I know plenty of well-educated people who have been fired. I also know amazingly untalented, not-very-smart people who have kept their jobs when others around them are being fired. There is no blueprint for this experience; the world is full of uncertainty and being fired is another experience you have limited control over. You can work hard, commit yourself in blood to your employer and still find yourself out in the cold. This is life.

Why is it important that we understand this? Because when you're fired it is all-too-easy to feel like you've failed and with this feeling of failure comes a sense of shame. We live in a world where for the most part failure is discouraged and therefore we feel ashamed if it is something we experience. And yet in reality we have nothing at all to feel ashamed about.

WHAT DID YOU FAIL AT TODAY?

Shame is an emotion that almost everyone I have ever spoken to about this topic has experienced. On both occasions of being fired, shame was one of the first things I felt. I was ashamed to tell my family and friends what had happened. Ashamed to use the word 'fired' and ashamed to talk about it with anyone, even strangers. And yet I knew I had done nothing wrong. I couldn't have worked harder or given more to both jobs. I had nothing to be ashamed about and yet that is exactly how I felt. I think this has to change. We need to change the stigma attached to being fired so that 'shame' is not the first emotion we feel. Knowing that you are in good company when it comes to being fired is a great place to start.

In the world of business and celebrity, there is a long list of people who credit being fired or rejected with their ultimate success in the world. J.K. Rowling was an unemployed single mother when she began writing the first Harry Potter book. Oprah Winfrey was fired from her first TV job as anchor in Baltimore. Steven Spielberg was rejected twice from the University of Southern California School of Cinematic Arts. Stephen King had his first book rejected 30 times before someone finally agreed to publish it. The list is endless.

The difference between these people who have gone on to have incredible success in their lives and careers and the average person is simply in the way they approach failure. They come back fighting. They take the opportunity to build the life they really want and experience more success than they could ever have achieved if they had not been pushed. They take failure and make it the foundation with which they build their future success.

For the most part the shame stems from how we have been bought up. The majority of parents, with all their love and support, want to keep us protected from the pain of the world. They don't want to see us experiencing the hurt, suffering or anxiety that comes with major failure so they keep us wrapped in cotton wool and then send us off into the world hoping that we'll continue to grow and succeed but never fail. Unfortunately the world we live in is not like this and this sets our children up for great disappointment and an inability to cope with the failures of life.

Modern-day schools are a great example of this. When I was growing up it tended to be only parents that tried to protect us from failure but now schools and teachers are trying to do the same thing. These days, schools hand out awards not to the most talented, the hardest working or the brightest child, but to the whole class for just turning up. Such is the need to avoid making one child feel like a failure.

A colleague recently told me that the policy at her child's school was that birthday parties thrown for students must include an invitation to the entire class, so no child feels left out. Having once been the only kid in a class not to be invited to a birthday party, I can tell you that this does not do these children any favours. Being excluded from that birthday party when I was ten years old gave me a good taste for what the world is really like. There are no blanket invitations in life. Some people like us, some people don't; it's inevitable. And so failure at times is inevitable. We are not helping our children by shielding them from the failures of life.

The father of Sara Blakely who founded women's underwear brand Spanx, certainly did not support this notion of shielding his children from failure. In a recent interview, Blakely spoke about how her father would ask her every evening, 'What did you fail at today?' Instead of berating her and telling her to try harder, her father would high-five her and congratulate her when she recognised where she had failed. Her father's approach to failure was that if you were not failing daily, you were not doing enough to push yourself out of your comfort zone.

Blakely grew up believing it was important to try new things and that it was okay to fail as long as you used the failure to build the base of your success. She was unafraid to push the boundaries of what she was capable of, believing that failure is something that deserves a high-five, not something to be avoided. It is unsurprising then that Blakely went on to become the youngest self-made female billionaire in the world.

IT'S REALLY VERY NORMAL

If failure is an inevitable part of life then understanding that being fired can happen to any one of us is an important concept to grasp. The more you talk about being fired, the more normal it becomes. If you scratch the surface a huge number of people you know will have been touched by it personally usually when they have lost their own job. In this modern world of economic uncertainty being fired is an everyday occurrence. Having a job today, does not mean you will have a job tomorrow; there are no guarantees.

I recently read an article in London's Evening Standard asking young people about their attitude towards the future and how optimistic they felt. A young couple was interviewed for the article and the boyfriend responded by saying 'we are comfortable and have disposable income so we are happy about the future. My job is secure and [my girlfriend] is happy at home'.

'My job is secure'? That seemed like a very bold statement to be making on the front cover of the Evening Standard. I continued to wonder for the rest of the evening just what it was about his job that gave this young man so much confidence that it was 'secure'. Either he was incredibly optimistic or like me at the same age, incredibly naïve. If you had asked my 24-year-old self if her job was secure, I would have given you a dumb look and said 'of course'. It never really occurs to us in our early twenties that we can be smart, talented and very good at our jobs, and still in line to be fired.

More often than not people are fired simply because they are not the right fit for the company they are working for. It is for this reason that it is important not to take losing your job personally, as contradictory as that may sound. There are some places you will fit in and some places you wont. Surely it is so much better to find a place where you do fit!

The perfect place for one person may be hell for another. I've worked at places where I fitted in perfectly and others where I was completely out of place. Two of the places I didn't fit in, fired me. Not because I wasn't good, but because I wasn't right for them. I liken it to being in a bad relationship. You try really hard to make it work, even if you know it's not right and when it finally does end, it breaks your heart because you tried so hard. But when you look back years later, you smile and think 'wow, what was I so upset about?' Being fired for not being the right fit is exactly like that.

Unsurprisingly, probationary periods are one of the most common times that people are fired from their job. Research suggests that close to 20% of all people fail their probation period and it's not a difficult statistic to believe. The interview process is all about the right qualifications and skills and impressing potential employers with the perfect answer to all the probing questions. However most traditional interview situations fail to account for ensuring the interviewee and the company are a good match. Everyone is so focused on impressing each other that the hard questions sometimes don't get asked. Then during the first three months of the job the reality starts to show. Once the honeymoon period is over, you start to realise that maybe you are not as perfect for each other as you thought!

It will probably be hard to believe at first, but in hindsight you will be able to recognize the situation and your limitations within it. It's important that you look back at the experience and understand the reasons you may have been fired. You will need this rational evaluation as you move forward into new opportunities. Knowing why things ended and closing the door on this chapter will leave the space open for you to move forward with a clear head, ready to excel with new opportunities.

TURN YOUR HEAD TO THE WIND AND NEVER LOOK BACK

The interesting thing about being fired is the mix of emotions we feel. We are all unique individuals so our reactions will never be identical but it's fairly common to experience a mix of anger, resentment, fear, frustration, denial, hatred, shock and of course, shame. Being fired, like so many other life-changing experiences brings up the most challenging of emotions.

All these emotions are completely normal and understandable reactions to a tough situation. You may not feel them all at once but you will probably feel most of them at some point. You will no doubt go through some sort of cycle: one day you will feel anger, the next day you will feel sadness and later you will feel regret. It is all part of the process.

In her book *High Octane Women: How Superachievers Can Avoid Burnout*, psychologist Sherrie Bourg Carter explains that many people link their occupations to their overall identity. It is common for the emotions surrounding losing a job to be similar to the grief experienced when losing a loved one.

Carter advises that you should seek the help of a professional if the emotions are becoming overwhelming. 'It's normal to feel sad, in some cases very sad, after losing a job,' she says. 'However, if the depression gets to the point where thoughts of suicide develop or the person is so depressed that they can't get out of bed or can't function effectively, then that is not normal.'

For me, it was never this bad. There were definitely some tough moments - more than I'd like to remember - but it never got quite as bad as this. It is sad to know that, for some people, the situation is so overwhelming that this is the reality.

It is for this reason I feel so passionately about changing the stigma that surrounds losing your job. You are not alone; it happens to the best of us and if you let it, you will see there is huge opportunity in the experience. We live in a society that tells us it is not ok to fail. Yet here we are, surrounded by individuals who failed and went on to experience great success, many of them when they were fired from a job. There is an abundance of opportunity in the experience of losing your job. Embrace it and you will see that life can be even more amazing than you thought.

KEY LESSONS FROM CHAPTER 2:

- Failure, such as when you are fired is much more common than you might first think. Some of the world's most successful people have become so, in part, because they were fired or failed in a major way. Failure should be embraced!

- In our modern economy being fired has become increasingly common. Once you start talking about it, you will soon discover that more people than you realise have been fired and lived to tell the tale.

- Embracing failure and the role it plays in our successes is an important part of moving forward after being fired.

CHAPTER 3:
FIRED WITH DIGNITY

Sometimes you just have to smile, pretend everything is okay and walk away.

Unknown

While it may be very normal in today's world to be fired or made redundant, it is still human nature to feel angry and betrayed. Unfortunately, the truth of the matter is as soon as you walk out the door your company has forgotten about you and you should do the same. Bitterness, anger and resentment are the worst of traits even at the best of times but spending the next 12 months telling everyone who will listen (and some who won't!) about how you've been wronged and how awful your former employers are will not win you any friends. Sure, vent your frustration for the first few weeks. It's okay to feel these emotions but then park them and move on; for the sake of your family and your friends but most of all for yourself. There is nothing to be achieved by holding onto anger and resentment. The sooner you let it go the quicker you will move on to the incredible new life that lies before you. Carrying all that baggage just slows you down.

STAY DIGNIFIED

The best way to dump the baggage from this awful experience is to hold it together and maintain your self-respect. It will take every ounce of your self-control and go against every emotion you are feeling but I can assure you, the best way to move on at speed is to be fired with your dignity intact.

I understand it might be an oxymoron putting 'fired' and 'dignity' in the same sentence but from experience I can tell you it is possible and you will feel one hundred times better if you act with class.

I didn't get this entirely right the first time. Bursting into tears at the announcement of my termination was definitely not in line with the classy self I am advocating you become. Although the awkwardness that ensued was enough to convince my boss that one-month gardening leave was a good idea! Nor was dashing into the pub with mascara-stained cheeks a brilliant idea. I did however, walk back into the office on the Monday morning with my head held high. I could have refused to come back in, refused to hand over the projects I was working on and refused to speak to my boss. But I didn't.

For me it was important to hold myself together in the face of adversity and you should do the same. Do you really want to be the crazy lady standing at the door shouting obscenities across the office? Or the tough guy who becomes aggressive and starts throwing punches? Or, even worse, the person who takes to social media to vent their anger for the whole of the cyberworld to see?

Don't be that person.

As Harvard professor Rosabeth Moss Kanter so eloquently put it in the Harvard Business Review, 'Try to die with dignity (career-wise), because you will be resuscitated and rehabilitated faster if you do.'

No matter what happens, try to maintain some level of dignity in the face of humiliation and embarrassment. It will be completely incongruous with the natural feelings you are experiencing but it is important. No matter how upset you are, try to limit emotional outpourings to the privacy of your own home or the shoulder of a friend. Not in the office, not in the face of your boss and definitely not on social media.

It will not feel like it at first but there will be a moment in the not-too-distant future where you will no longer feel the anger or resentment that you feel right now. It is in this moment that you will either thank your former self for maintaining dignity in the face of humiliation or find your cheeks burning with shame.

The simple fact is no one will thank you for throwing your 'toys out of the pram' and behaving like a child. Your colleagues, who will be left to pick up your work, will be frustrated at not knowing what you were working on and your boss will feel vindicated in the decision to let you go. Holding your head high with dignity is the only way to ensure the respect you deserve.

The second time I was fired, I was determined not to let my boss 'win'. I wasn't going to let the humiliation of the situation define the way I behaved. I wanted to be bigger than this, even though inside I was curled up in the foetal position wishing it would all go away.

I was fired on a Friday and did not tell anyone I knew over the weekend. It was one of the loneliest weekends of my life. I was too scared and humiliated to admit what had happened. Maybe it was out of shock more than anything but I decided that the best course of action was to 'keep calm and carry on'. I had a one-week notice period to work through and I was going to stay until the end.

It sounds crazy to almost everyone I tell but my main motivation for working through my notice period was to show my boss and my former colleagues what a classy individual they were losing. I did not want there to be a single opportunity to observe that the decision to let me go was the right one.

No one had expected me to work through my notice period but those who were due to pick up my workload were extremely grateful. All week I had people come to my desk to tell me how impressed they were that I had showed up. Every time someone said that to me I wanted to cry. On the inside I was petrified but on the outside I kept it together for all to see.

WALKING THE WALK

In many cases after being fired there are no expectations of the fired employee returning to work. For reasons unique to each company, they may 'walk' you from the building on the spot. No chance to say goodbye or get your personal belongings. They just walk you straight out the door.

I have been very lucky not to have this happen to me but have heard from those who have, that it can be an incredibly humiliating experience. Being marched through the office and out the door like a criminal only adds to what is already an awful situation. I can imagine that when this happens it feels impossible to keep things together. My advice however remains the same; do everything you can to make a dignified exit.

A close friend was in charge of a company that was struggling financially. Over the course of a year they were forced to make significant redundancies and he was the guy who had to walk those people from the building. Everyone's reaction was different. Some people were in shock and said nothing, many women cried and one guy reacted so badly he threw a punch! As you can imagine, nobody regretted making him redundant.

As fate would have it the company was struggling so badly that later that year they also made my friend redundant. The same waves of anger, resentment, and humiliation washed over him.

However, in the days that followed he decided not to let his emotions override the situation. He emailed his former boss and the CEO to thank them for the opportunities they had given him. A week later he followed up on his email with a visit to his former office where he gave his boss a hug and told her that she shouldn't feel guilty or upset at firing him. It's not hard to imagine the reaction this got.

Feeling compassion for the person who has fired you is very difficult, but incredible if you can do it. Often the person firing you has no choice. In the very least, they will not enjoy the experience and they will enjoy even less being the person who has to walk you out the door. If you can't muster up compassion for them, as a bare minimum hold your head high and behave with dignity. Everyone will love you for it.

REMEMBER THIS

It is difficult in the midst of being fired to remember all the reasons it's so important to hold it together. So here are my top three:

1. **Reputation**

   Most industries are small, even in big cities like London. People talk, stories get spread. Bad behaviour when you are fired will follow you to subsequent jobs, as will good behaviour. Knowing you stayed professional when faced with humiliation will speak volumes about you as a future employee of a new company. Added to which, people move companies with frequency these days. You would hate to find that a former colleague or boss who witnessed your bad behaviour, now works for a company you wish to be employed by.

2. **Severance**

   The compensation you receive when being fired should be as black and white as the contract you signed. But more often than not human compassion will kick in and an employer will do what they can to soften the blow: either financially or through making the situation more comfortable. I have experienced this on both occasions. The first time, my boss allowed me four weeks paid leave so I would not have to work through my notice period. The second time, my boss financially compensated me in excess of what was required in my contract (it was Christmas after all!). Both acts of kindness I received were in part due to the professionalism I showed.

3. You'll just feel so good!

Having done it twice myself I can promise you that nothing will feel better than knowing what a kick-ass professional you are! Looking back you will be high-fiving yourself and doing a dance inside knowing you were the one who kept their cool. At a time when you have lost most of your confidence knowing how awesome you can be in the face of adversity will make you feel amazing!

And it is this ability to hold yourself together that will lay the foundation for the incredible new life that lies ahead. It won't feel like it at the time but the journey you are about to embark on can take you to a place far better than where you started. But you have to believe that it really is an opportunity. You need to look at what has happened with a rational head and reframe all the negative thoughts and emotions you are experiencing. It's not easy, but it will be worth it.

KEY LESSONS FROM CHAPTER 3

- Being fired with dignity is the best antidote for surviving the experience. As hard as it may seem, controlling your emotions and keeping a rational head when you're fired is much better than yelling or crying (at least in front of your boss and colleagues).

- Often bad news travels fast within an industry. Holding your head high and walking out of the situation with dignity will help to resuscitate your career much faster than behaving badly and dragging the situation out.

- Your reputation, severance package and your own mental health are practical reasons why behaving calmly and rationally is the best way forward when you are fired.

CHAPTER 4:
REFRAMING YOUR STORY

Whether you think you can, or you think you can't – you're right.

Unknown

When I first told people I was writing a book about being fired the reaction from most people was one of scepticism. People who were unaware I'd lost my job twice were often shocked to hear this news. In some instances I genuinely believe they thought I was lying. People would look at the success I'd had in my career and wrongly assume that I was not the type of person who could ever be fired.

The negative connotations of being fired are so ingrained in our society that the idea that someone who is confident and successful can be fired from a job is hard to comprehend. We associate being fired with the lazy, the socially-awkward or people who lie about their skill set. In reality, being fired can happen to any of us, even the most talented, the hardest working or the most well-educated. You can call it whatever politically correct term you want: laid off, given notice, made redundant, dismissed. It's all the same. You were fired.

I have been made redundant twice and I have been fired twice. Whilst the former experience is usually softened by the knowledge that you are being fired en masse, it is still a type of firing none the less. I know this because after I had been made redundant, on both occasions I was offered a new job with the company. That was not true for everyone who was made redundant; if a company wants to keep you they'll find a way.

Now, I can appreciate that in some cases companies genuinely need to let staff go due to forces beyond their control. And in this case I concede that perhaps your company did not have a choice. However, the result is the same. You very suddenly find the rug pulled out from under you and life changes in an instant.

So why when we know that being fired can happen to anyone of us do we continue to attach such negative beliefs to the experience? If some of the brightest, smartest, most talented people we know have been fired shouldn't we stop to consider the role that being fired has ultimately played in their future success?

In a now very famous commencement speech that Steve Jobs gave at Stanford University in 2005, he acknowledged that being fired from Apple was actually a good thing. In hindsight, it took being fired from his own company to take him into an incredibly creative period of his life; one where he created businesses such as Pixar and he was so successful he was eventually re-hired by Apple.

Whether you are being fired from a billion-dollar technology company or from a small accounting firm, the situation is always the same. The way you choose to react will determine the success you have in the months and years that follow. The story you tell yourself in your head will ultimately be the reality you create. You can be like Steve Jobs and seize the opportunity to create a new path to success, or you can let it sink you; the choice is always your own.

CREATING A NEW STORY

In the days and weeks after losing your job it is important to take the time to consider what has just happened. There is always a period of shock; a time where you simply cannot get your head around what has happened. But as this feeling starts to subside, you need to get your story straight in your own mind. Remember you can spin a story any way you like. As the quote says, 'whether you think you can, or you think you can't – you're right'. It's all in your head so make the story a good one.

The first time I was fired, it was very easy for me to reframe the experience. I was young. My expectations of life were pretty low at that point so I was able to bounce back fairly quickly. I reasoned with myself that the job I had just lost was as planned, my 'starter' job in London; I never intended it to be long-term. In fact it was well below the expectations I had for myself when I moved half way around the world. It was time to move onto the next stage of my London career and start to build the life I had come all this way for.

But my second firing was much more emotional. It took a huge amount of soul searching and deep thinking to ensure the story I told myself was a positive one. It didn't happen straight away. For the first few weeks, I was in denial and the weeks after that I was simply miserable. As I started to come round, I realised I needed to really digest what had happened if I was going to move on with my life. I did not want the baggage of this situation to be following me around forever.

So I sat down one afternoon and wrote down every thought I could about the job I'd lost and the situation I found myself in. It was difficult bringing back up all the emotions. Denial is a much easier place to be in the short term but once it all started spilling out on the paper it was clear that this situation whilst not ideal, was probably the best outcome longer-term. From my first day at that job I had never really felt part of the company or the team. I had not connected with a single one of my workmates, nor did I have any desire to. By the end I was trying my hardest to do well but daily I was having my confidence knocked in every direction. The more my confidence was affected the worse I performed and the more miserable I became. It was a downward spiral that I have seen many people fall into. Once your confidence goes it is very difficult to find your way back.

In my heart I knew that being fired was the quickest and easiest way to send me back to the path I was meant to be on. I didn't know where that path was leading but I had to trust that the universe knew where I was going.

So I reframed the story in my head. Instead of focusing on the negative (hating people I worked with and despising my former boss), I chose to focus on the opportunities that were open to me now.

Taking the job I had just been fired from was a risk in the first place. I left a job I loved to take this new role for no other reason than I felt like my life needed a shake-up. I had become too comfortable - bordering on complacent - and I needed a change. Well, I got what I was looking for. My world had been disrupted on a scale I had never experienced before! The story I told myself was that when the dust settled life would be amazing again. There was no other choice. I could tell myself that I had failed, that life was a disaster and my world was over, but what good would that do? If you can choose the story you tell yourself every day, why would you make the story anything other than positive?

Seeing my unemployment as a massive opportunity to learn and grow was the only way to ensure the sadness of the situation did not envelope me. It kept my head above ground and helped me make positive, rational steps toward the new life I was dreaming of. Getting the story straight in my head was the most important part of making this happen.

The world of redundancy and job loss is full of success stories. Facing adversity requires you to dig deeper than you have before and call on strength you never knew you had. When the adversity faced is that of losing a job it forces you to question your life choices, open up to new opportunities and ultimately reassess exactly what it is you want from life.

When you connect the threads of your life you will see how everything fits back together but it's impossible to know how the threads connect in the future. Only when you look back on your past will you see the role these events played in your life and how important it was that you reframed the opportunity you were given.

WE BECOME THE STORIES WE TELL OURSELVES

Learning to reframe the stories you have in your head will have an incredible impact on the results you see in your life. Have you ever wondered how two children can grow up in the same house, have the same experiences and yet view those experiences through a completely different lens? That's because with every experience in life we choose the way we react to it. There are always a million different ways to create a story in your head and you are the only person who decides what that story will be. The story becomes the truth because you believe it.

I learnt this lesson in a very powerful way years ago, when I was on my first ever personal development course. The course leader was talking to us about the stories in our head, and how we create the story we tell ourselves. A young Asian man stood up at the microphone to recount a story from his childhood and how it had shaped his adult belief that the world is full of racism. The man recalled an incredibly sad story about being seven years old and having his family's Asian takeaway shop attacked by white supremacists. The family home was above the takeaway shop and he remembered huddling in the corner of his bedroom with his mother whilst these men threw Molotov cocktails through the front of the store. It was incredibly sad and the man welled up as he recounted what was obviously an incredibly painful experience.

As he finished and declared that life as an Asian was tough because the world was full of racism, illustrated perfectly by the attack on his family's store, the course leader asked him to recall other details of the night. As it turned out, the young man had suppressed many details in a way that helped to validate the story he was telling himself about racism in the world.

As the course leader delved deeper into the man's memory, it soon became clear that this attack on his family's store was not at all racially motivated. The attackers were not white supremacists at all; in fact it was not just the Asian takeaway that was attacked that night. Ten other buildings in the street were set alight, many of them owned by white people.

Somewhere along the line, this man had decided to create a story in his head about race and use the experience of that night to validate the story he was telling himself. In the end it emerged that the attack was nothing to do with race. He had spent his whole life believing the world was against him because of his skin colour and as it turns out he had created that reality only in his own head.

Just like the man in this story we all run the risk of creating a reality of half-truths. We decide what it is we want the story to be and we create a new narrative in our heads that validates the story we want to create. It is a dangerous place to be. You could soon find yourself believing something about yourself or the world around you that is simply not true.

It is important to assess the story you are telling yourself when you are fired. There is so much emotion at play that it's difficult to see the rational world. But it doesn't help to validate a story that suggests you are not good at your job or there is some sort of conspiracy against you. You have to create a story that sets you up for success.

DON'T MISS THE STORY RIGHT IN FRONT OF YOU

One of the most common and challenging instances of job loss is amongst middle-aged men. For all the pressures that besiege women – trying to be the perfect mother, wife and employee – men are faced with their own set of pressures that perhaps the world doesn't acknowledge enough. Perhaps its men themselves that won't acknowledge them but either way, by the time men reach middle age, many have started to lose their way even if they don't know it yet.

The Samaritans suicide report of 2016 shows that men aged 45-49 are the demographic most likely to commit suicide. This rate is almost four times that of women the same age. As a society we spend an extraordinary amount of airtime discussing the social pressures faced by women, yet we almost forget that men are suffering too. If I thought being fired was tough at 32, with no kids or real responsibilities it's hard to imagine what it must be like for a 45-year-old father of three. Not only does he have the added worry of how to provide for his family, but losing his job is a considerable blow to his masculinity.

Steve Biddulph's 'Manhood' is a fascinating read (for both genders) into the life of a man. In this book, Biddulph talks about men being trapped in their jobs, forced to wait until retirement for the life they really want. In the interim, men become miserable, living a life they did not plan for themselves. For me, most interesting are his thoughts on the middle-aged man. Bidduplh declares, 'Our marriages fail, our kids hate us, we die of stress and on the way, we destroy the world.' After reading this book I wanted to give every middle-aged man I knew a hug!

So how does a 45-year-old father reframe the experience of being fired? I can imagine it's pretty tough. I was lucky that in both cases of being fired it was only me that I had to look out for. The added pressure of providing for a family was not something I had to deal with. But when it comes to reframing the story your family are the ideal motivation to help propel you forward. Losing your job yet still being surrounded by a loving family should be all the proof you need that even when you hit rock bottom there is still a reason to get up every day.

A few years ago, an acquaintance of mine found himself in this exact situation. An ambitious over-achiever, he'd found success fairly easy to come by in his early career. By no means undeserved – he worked incredibly hard – he simply found that the career ladder continued to go up and up. The more success came to him, the harder he worked and the more hours he spent away from his family. The sad reality of success amongst middle-aged men it seems is that the first place to suffer is the home. His impressive six-figure salary ensured that his wife had no cause for complaint about the lifestyle they lived but inevitably he was disconnected from his family and their day-to-day life. Then one day, completely out of the blue, he was fired. Walked unceremoniously from the building, he found himself lying on the couch smelling of beer by the time his five-year-old got home from school.

As he contemplated the next stage of his career, he was simultaneously thrust back into the role of domestic caregiver. His wife worked and was now the sole breadwinner. His new role involved getting his children dressed, fed and off to school, as well as picking them up and organising after-school activities. It was a role he was completely unfamiliar with and by his own admission, involved a set of skills he simply didn't have. More worryingly for him, it involved a set of relationships he didn't have either. In the corporate world he could make a phone call and get what he needed by leveraging one of hundreds of business relationships he had made over the course of his career. But at home, his relationships with the little people in his life were virtually non-existent. The hardest part of being fired it would seem, was not the need to find another job but instead the spotlight it shone on the gulf between him and his children.

It was this realisation that forced my friend to reframe his firing. For the first few months he wallowed in self-pity. His thoughts were occupied with feelings of anger towards his former employer coupled with fear about where he would end up next. When his five-year-old declared one afternoon that she was happy he had lost his job because she 'loved afternoons with Daddy', a light bulb finally came on in his head. He suddenly realised that far from being the life-ending experience he was framing it up to be being fired was a magical opportunity. He could spend his time feeling sorry for himself and telling himself how unjustly he had been treated, or he could get busy capitalising on the incredible position he now found himself in.

Suffice to say, family life improved considerably. And while it took him eight months to find himself a new job, he enjoyed the journey. When he finally did go back to work it was on his terms - terms that worked for him AND his family.

Being fired is one of the best opportunities you will have to reframe a situation so that the outcome will be favourable. Like my own story or that of my friend, our reality is shaped by the stories we believe. If you believe that being fired is the worst experience of your life and that you will never recover from it then this will most likely become your reality – until you change your mind. If (or when) you choose to embrace the opportunity the world will open up for you. The difference between successful people and the rest of the world is the way they choose to explain their failures to themselves. Re-framing the 'failure' of being fired will set you on course for the next hugely successful chapter in your life.

KEY LESSONS FROM CHAPTER 4:

- Reframing the story in your head is incredibly important if you are going to move forward and build an amazing new life. Dwelling on what happened and the negative emotions of the situation will keep you trapped in the past.

- The stories we tell ourselves are what we believe, and we become these stories. If you can choose the story you tell yourself why not make it a positive one?

- Sometimes there is an amazing opportunity to reframe a situation right in front of us. Don't miss the opportunity by focusing on the wrong things.

CHAPTER 5:
YOU'VE GOTTA HAVE A PLAN

A fool with a plan can outsmart a genius with no plan.

T. Boone Pickens

January 2014 was without doubt one of the worst months of my life. The Christmas holidays had managed to mask the emotions of being fired for the second time. A wonderful Christmas break to Berlin, followed by four days in Krakow, provided the perfect blanket with which to cover my anger, fear, and sadness. But arriving back in London on New Year's Day delivered the sobering reality of my new life; tomorrow was January 2nd and I had nowhere to be.

Somewhere on the other side of the world it was summer. The sun was shining, barbeques were being cooked, my friends and family were together and life was wonderful. Losing my job, coupled with my inevitable homesickness for the southern hemisphere, sent me into a downward spiral that even now I can't explain. I had lost my confidence along with the reason I got out of bed every day. I would literally wake up in the morning, look out the window and draw a blank as to how I would spend my day.

For the most part, I can't tell you how I spent my days back in January 2014. Of course, I was calling recruiters, writing my CV, contacting old colleagues and generally going through the motions of looking for a job but I couldn't really tell you what my purpose was. I was running on desperation, watching the days of the month tick away like a time bomb. Every day that passed, I cursed and berated myself for still being unemployed. I was trying so hard to get my old life back that I was missing the opportunity that lay in front of me: the opportunity to create a new one.

CREATING A LIFELINE

As January drew to a close and I was no closer to employment than when I flew back from Poland at the start of the month, it began to dawn on me that being fired might actually be the best thing that could have happened at that time.

The empty January days had provided me with the chance to reflect on my life and the circumstances that had got me to where I was that day. Despite loving my job for most of my twenties, something was always missing. I could never quite put my finger on it. In the back of my mind I knew I wanted more from life. By January 2014 life as I knew it was gone and it was time to take back control.

Years ago I was watching an episode of the reality TV show *The Biggest Loser* (don't judge me!). The show is a competition between overweight individuals all competing to lose the most amount of weight in a specified time period. They are supported with trainers, nutritionists and psychologists on a private estate. Then towards the end of the show they are let back out into their former lives to see if they can continue to lose weight using the techniques they have been taught. As far as reality TV goes, it's a fairly fascinating insight into human struggles and everyday life challenges.

It was getting to about the halfway point in the series and there was a conversation between one of the trainers and one of the contestants. They were having an in-depth discussion about how to win the competition, when the trainer told the contestant, 'You've gotta have plan. Every person who has ever won this show, had a plan'.

Given that I personally considered reality TV to be shallow and demeaning, this one statement had a hugely profound effect on me. At the time, I had just been made redundant and was trying to figure out what to do with my life. I was 30 years old and having lived in the UK for my entire working life I was considering a move home to New Zealand for the first time. I was also considering taking another job with the company that had made me redundant as well as going travelling (always a great fall back), moving to a new foreign country or finding a different job in London. I had no idea what I wanted to do and I was completely unable to make a decision.

The struggle I had was that I didn't really know what I was trying to achieve with my life. I wasn't unhappy but if you had questioned my values and tried to work out how they aligned to my overall life plan you would have discovered very quickly that I was just living life as it came.

I was a hard worker, I found satisfaction in a job well done. I had enjoyed plenty of success in my career, so on the surface it probably looked as though I had a very clear direction. The truth was, while I'd take opportunities as they arose, I wasn't really pushing my life in any direction that I had consciously mapped out for myself.

So when I heard the trainer on *The Biggest Loser* profess that every single winner of the show (at that stage in its 8th season) had had a plan for winning, I was shocked. I had watched the show for years and frankly just thought that the contestants were a bunch of individuals who had clearly let life get the better of them. Hearing that amongst this bunch at least one always had a clear plan for winning gave me a whole new appreciation for the show, for its contestants and for the need to have a plan in my life.

Whenever I speak to friends or coaching clients about having a plan, their main objection stems from thinking that a plan is some sort of rigid framework for life. Most people wrongfully assume that having a plan involves sacrifice and willpower. The ironic delight experienced by most is that, rather than keeping you chained up, a plan is incredibly liberating. There is something very refreshing about knowing where you are going and what you are doing. It releases the brain from the daily angst of trying to work out if it's on the right track and is a source of comfort when you need it most.

Having a clear plan for your life is an essential tool for everyone but having a clear plan when you've been fired is like giving yourself a lifeline. A plan helps provide direction and focus. It means that on those days when all you want to do is stay in bed and feel sorry for yourself, you get up and attack the day. Why? Because you don't have to spend the first 30 minutes of the day working out why you are getting out of bed today. You have already consciously decided where you want to go and how you are going to get there, so each day simply becomes another day on the path to where you are going. On a day-to-day basis, it doesn't require a lot of thought. You have already agreed the plan with yourself, so you just need to get up and execute it.

ALL GREAT SUCCESS COMES WITH A PLAN

Not long after the *'Biggest Loser'* revelation when I started scratching the surface of my friends' lives I realised that every successful person I know has a plan. People like to tell you that they don't, as if they are afraid to admit that they went out and worked hard for something. But if you delve deeper and ask the right questions, you'll soon realise that the most successful people you know do not become so by just floating through life. Whether they committed their plan to paper, computer or their brain, it exists. Even if it is not 12 pages long, even if it's just one single determined focus to achieve something, it is still a plan.

I recently had the pleasure of attending a course run by Lindsay Hopkins, the author of *'Step Up and FOCUS'* which highlights the importance of goal setting. Lindsay is an incredibly successful businessman, property investor and personal coach. During the course he spent a couple of hours talking to us about making plans to achieve our goals. We discussed Mind Mapping, pulling together plans and reviewing our goals. It was all stuff I had heard before until Lindsay offered up physical examples of his own personal goal-setting documents for us to read. 11 years worth of Mind Maps and goal planning books, mapped out across all aspects of life! Financial, business, investment, family, friends, fitness, well-being, community… you name it, Lindsay had a goal for it.

I was frankly quite stunned. I had written goals of my own over the years (usually on the back of an envelope) but had never seen anything on this scale. Truth is, I had never seen the goals or planning of a successful individual like Lindsay. It had never occurred to me that incredibly successful people have such detailed plans behind their success; I just assumed they were simply more talented than the rest of us. Could it really be that they are just more focused and know the roadmap for where they want to go?

If you ask Lindsay, that's exactly what he will tell you. Luck and talent has very little to do with it. Planning, focus and perseverance is what sets the successful apart from the rest.

One of my former colleagues used to write a yearly keynote presentation with his goals for the year. Every December, he would draft his plan, and by New Year's Eve it would be finished. The same way we would write strategic business plans for the company, he would set up his goals for his life. Objectives, strategy, key drivers… it was a full-on life plan with specific detail of how he would get where he wanted to be.

He shared it with me one day towards the end of the year when we were discussing a major life event that had just taken place for him. 'It was in my plan', he said, before confessing that he writes a keynote every year with his goals. Sure enough, the life event that had just taken place was there in his plan for the year along with a million other things he had already achieved.

Unsurprisingly, this friend went on to be one of the most successful young talents to come out of the company. He worked for the global head office in the United States and held incredibly senior roles at a very young age - all of which were in his plan, of course. To the outside world it looked as if he had a lot of luck and the right people backing him but in fact luck had very little to do with it. He decided what he wanted, wrote it down and worked hard on it every single day. This is the power of having a plan.

TAKE BACK CONTROL

Writing a plan after being fired is often hard when you feel lost and unsure where life it taking you next. This is exactly the reason why writing one early in the process is so critical. You have already had the wind knocked out of your sails. Someone else has altered your path without your permission; now it is time to take back control.

Writing my own plan after losing my job for the second time was tough. I had been mentally wrecked by the experience so planning how to get myself back to a safe emotional state was just as important as deciding where I wanted my life to go next. I decided that any plan that was too stringent and robust was more likely to set me up to fail as my fragile state was not really equipped to deal with massive goal-setting and achievement. I needed a plan that would help to rebuild my confidence, bring joy back into my life and get me back out into the world.

The lesson I learnt from being fired twice was that my plan needed to have more 'me' and less 'work'. Life so far had been mainly focused on my job with little thought given to developing myself and pursuing the things I loved. Not that I didn't love my job – in actual fact, I've been very lucky and have genuinely enjoyed the majority of jobs in my career to date – it was just that I did not have a plan to grow other areas of my life.

When I sat down and thought about what needed developing, especially in light of losing my job for the second time, I came up with five areas of my life that I would develop. I called these my Life PLANS, standing for:

P – Passions
L – Loved Ones
A – Activity
N – Network
S – Soul

I decided that instead of writing a keynote presentation on how to get a new job I would create focus around these five areas. They were not directly related to getting a job but I realised that if I succeeded in these areas I would be happier, healthier and ultimately the job would become a by-product of this plan. I didn't need to focus on the job; I needed to focus on rebuilding myself and creating the life that I really wanted. The job, I realised, would take care of itself.

In his book, *The Score Takes Care of Itself*, Bill Walsh talks of the culture and ethos he instilled at the San Francisco 49ers in the year before they went from the worst team in the NFL to Super Bowl champions. Walsh was in charge of the team at the time and decided that instead of focusing on winning games, the focus would be on setting a new standard within the franchise that everyone from the receptionist to the quarterback would follow. His thinking was that as long as they were focusing on getting all the basics right the score would take care of itself.

For an example of a PLANS planning template, visit www.lifeafterfired.com/resources

This is the approach of Life PLANS: focus on building yourself, and the right job will emerge. Focus on getting the basics right in all areas of your personal development is the first step towards an amazing new life, one that you created and is under your control. Identifying and developing these five areas of your life will ensure that you hit unemployment at full speed, ready to crash through the barriers and come out the other side pumping and full of life.

KEY LESSONS FROM CHAPTER 5:

- 'You've gotta have a plan'. All the most successful people in the world have a plan of some sort. Having a plan enables you to wake up every day with clarity and purpose, understanding exactly where you are going.
- Being fired will make you feel like you have lost control. Having a plan, far from being restrictive, provides you with the control you need to take back your life. It is this control that will lay the foundation for rebuilding the life you really want.

PART II: PLANS

CHAPTER 6:
P IS FOR PASSION

When you recover or discover something that nourishes your soul and brings joy, care enough about yourself to make room for it in your life.

Jean Shinoda Bolen

The first focus of my plan for getting the basics right in my life was Passion. As children, we are passionate beings with passion for so many different things. Finger painting, riding bikes, singing songs… it's not hard to find a long list of things that a young child loves. Sadly, somewhere between childhood and adulthood our passions start to fall away. We no longer have the time or focus to continue to evolve our passions. Work and adult life take over and the things that bring us joy get side-lined for the things that make us money or provide us with security.

Yet, deep inside our love for these things never really goes away. It took being unemployed to force me to rediscover some of the great loves of my childhood, which is a shame. Now I urge anyone not to wait until your life falls apart before you take the time to rediscover your own. It's incredibly liberating and your passions will bring you a huge amount of joy once they are back in your life.

DO WHAT YOU LOVE

When I was a child I loved to write. At ten-years old I won a local writing competition with a story about a sick penguin being rescued by a Greenpeace worker, with the moral of the story being that we needed to be kinder to our planet. When I was 11, my teacher took me aside and asked me if I would like to dedicate more of my time to writing. We agreed that I could spend an extra three hours per week on writing and that she would help me with my stories. By the time I was a teenager I would write in my diary every day. Most of it was teenage angst – boys I 'loved', friends who hurt me, experiences I wished I could have - but in amongst this was some very poignant and thoughtful writing. I also used to write poetry. It wasn't exactly Walt Whitman, but some of it was really beautiful.

I still have all my teenage diaries today; I brought them back to the UK some years ago but it was during my unemployment, when I was really soul-searching, that they came back into my life. I remember a cold and miserable morning in January when I woke up with very little to do. There was a threatening sky over Canary Wharf, it was only two degrees and it was clear there was rain on the way. So I decided to spend the day at home.

I had a book of quotes in my bedside drawer, which I would pull out when I needed a pick-me-up - motivational quotes carry so much more meaning when you've been fired!

'Bad decisions make good stories.'
'Pain makes you stronger. Tears make you braver.'
'Don't wait for the storm to pass. Learn to dance in the rain.'

There was nothing new here. But underneath this book were three of my teenage diaries. I hadn't read them in years! I read through page after page of my 'tragic' yet poetic youth and a fire inside me was re-lit. These diaries were not just my way of raging against the world, they were my outlets for creativity and writing them had brought me so much joy. As I sat there on that cold January morning, reliving the memories of my 16-year-old self, I knew writing was something I needed back in my life.

Right then and there, I picked up my MacBook and started to write. Unsurprisingly, I had a lot to say. Every emotion, every worry, every sadness and frustration came tumbling out onto the screen. It was over a month since I had been fired and writing it down was the best therapy I had found so far.

So for the next few months, I continued to write. I committed to writing at least three times a week but as I fell back in love with writing I'd usually do more.

So where did it go? How was it that I had let writing fall out of my life? Reading back through my diaries, the entries got fewer and fewer when I went off to university. I tried to revive it again my first year out of university and did manage to write some touching pieces about my childhood friends but it didn't stick. As my career blossomed, my passion for writing had died.

So here I was at 32, rediscovering what it meant to have a passion.

I can't tell you enough how much this process helped me survive the following seven months of uncertainty and anxiety. Having a creative outlet that bought me joy was one of the few bright spots in an otherwise tough period in my life.

It is for this reason that Passion is one of the key areas of your life to focus on as part of your PLANS. Everyone has a passion inside them. Quite often it is something you loved as a child so looking back into your past is a good place to start.

A close friend of mine recently rediscovered her passion for acting after 25 years. As an immigrant from Turkey, she arrived in Australia at the age of seven, speaking very little English. In fact, whenever any of the Australian children tried to speak to her in English, her response was always 'My name is Burju', as this was all she knew how to say. Fitting into life in Australia presented its own challenges and as she assimilated herself into her new world, drama class became the place she felt most confident and happy.

Fast forward a quarter century and she has taken up acting classes again. Personally, I would run for the hills if forced to participate in an acting class, but not Burju. Instead, she found the same joy and happiness she remembered as a child. It was an environment she loved, and she was delighted to be back there again.

REDISCOVERING YOUR PASSION

Here's a simple exercise you can use if you are struggling to remember the things you loved as a child. Take out a sheet of paper. Close your eyes and focus on memories of your childhood. It can be any age but if you don't know where to start, try an age between five and ten years old. Even if it wasn't a full-blown passion yet, chances are a hint of a love for something will have been blossoming at this age.

Remember your friends. What games did you play together? What activities did you like when you played with friends after school? What classes did you like most? Did you have any particular talents that teachers liked to nurture? Remember happy moments. When did they occur? What were you doing? Who were you with?

As thoughts come to your mind write them down and quickly go back to your daydream. After about 10 minutes of memories and writing you should have a paper full of childhood thoughts. Somewhere in there you will find a passion or two.

Depending on the type of childhood you had it may be difficult to delve back into your youth but trust me, it will be worth it. The joys of our youth never go away, we just somehow manage to forget them as we grow up. Finding them again will bring you so much joy.

MAKING YOURSELF MEMORABLE

Of course, having a passion holds more benefit than simply giving you joy. Passions also come into their own when it comes to making yourself memorable in a tough job market. CVs these days are pretty much identical so it's hard to tell a potential employer why you are better than the next guy. You need something to set you apart, and that is where your passion really comes into it's own.

I recently experienced this first hand when chatting to an intern who had landed a coveted job working for one of the world's biggest technology companies. It would be fair to assume an internship at one of the world's most recognisable brands would be difficult to come by, so I asked this intern, 'What was it about you that set you apart?' With all the humility in the world, he struggled to answer. He told me how he had a great CV and had done well at University so far, but so what? Loads of people had done this.

So I probed deeper. It turned out he was hugely passionate about football. He had spent a gap year coaching football to kids in the favelas (urban slums) of Rio de Janeiro in Brazil. When he talked about the experience it instantly set him apart. He even had a YouTube video of himself being interviewed by Sky News. You could tell he had loved the experience but his passion for football didn't stop there. He also revealed that at age 17, during his final high school exams, he had written a book about the history of his local football club. He interviewed current and past players, managers and fans to write a compelling history of the club he loved. He published it and it is still on sale today in the Club Store.

Now that's a passion! You'd struggle to find many 17-year-olds who have written a book, let alone managed to get it published and on sale in their local football club. On top of that, he made £8,000 from the sales of his book and gave all the proceeds to charity. That's how your Passion makes you stand out.

BECOME A SHOW-STOPPER

Your passions do not have to involve teaching under privileged children on the other side of the world how to play football. Everyday, simple passions can still add an extra dimension that makes people look at you twice.

Asking 'what do you do?' is the most boring yet most common question people ask when meeting someone new. We all have a quick two-to-three-word answer for this question and 90% of the time the answer people give is just as dull. Then occasionally someone comes along with a show-stopping response.

'I'm an astronaut'
'I'm a race car driver'
'I'm the guy who drives the machine that tunnels under central London building Crossrail' (true story!)

Now these are impressive! It must be great to have a show-stopping answer but sadly 90% of jobs won't sound so good. There is not much you can do about that unless you plan to retrain as an astronaut but with a passion in your life you can suddenly make yourself a show-stopper! Having a passion tells people surprising things about you that make them think twice. There is nothing more untrue than thinking you know everything about a person, just because you know their job. A person becomes more interesting, more three dimensional when their passions are revealed.

I have a brilliant example of this right in my own family. My brother Charlie works laying data cables in schools and office buildings. He loves his job but it's hardly going to stop dinner conversation when he announces what he does. What does catch people's attention, however, is what he does when he's not at work. Charlie is a DJ. He has a regular Saturday night gig at a club in his hometown but also picks up various festival and party slots. Charlie absolutely loves music – he always has. He is an example of an adult who grew up without letting his childhood passions go.

But music isn't Charlie's only passion. When he is not working as a DJ or laying data cables, Charlie has a garden. Not like a few shrubs and bushes outside his house but a proper, full-grown, feed-a-family, Sunday-lunch style vegetable garden. He grows everything from courgettes and tomatoes to lettuce and kale. When Charlie comes home to our parents' house for Christmas his biggest concern is who will water his vegetable garden? He talks about his garden like it's his child – with excitement, warmth and love.

When Charlie tells people about his passions they literally stop talking mid-sentence. He's a fairly unassuming guy, so most people are not expecting him to come out and say he is a DJ. When he backs that up with talk of his vegetable garden – a passion usually reserved for 60-year-old men – people always do a double-take. Here's this cool young guy who lays data cables for a living, moonlights as a DJ and spends his weekends watering his veggie garden – it's just too much for some people to get their head around!

DISCOVER SOMETHING NEW

If you can't find a passion from your childhood, there is no better time than during unemployment to find something new to enjoy. Finding a recreational hobby that lifts your spirits and makes you feel alive again is just what you need when you've lost your job. Looking for a new role may feel like a full-time job but the reality is you will struggle to fill a 40-hour week with a job hunt alone. In the downtime, you will need something to fill the void.

If you live in a big city a quick search on the Internet will show up thousands of opportunities to learn new skills or activities. Even in small towns there are usually still plenty of options. Such has our desire to pursue passions outside of working hours increased, a whole industry has risen to service our needs. You can learn tango dancing, creative writing, painting, sewing, take guitar lessons, learn a language... the opportunities are endless. If it wasn't something you had passion for as a child, never mind. Just find something that excites you and get involved.

For example, my housemate sings in a choir. They practice every Monday evening and give concerts to the local community twice a year at one of the coolest restaurants in East London. Forget your visions of a boring church choir; this choir is packed with cool creative people who love to sing, and see choir as an amazing place for creative release. They sing music mash-ups - not just modern pop songs, but new twists on old tunes. Think Whoopi Goldberg in Sister Act 2, taking something that could be very mainstream and making it exciting and fun.

The choir only performs twice a year and they don't get paid. So why do they turn up every Monday after work to sing with no audience? Because they love it - it's their passion! My housemate often sings in her room during the week as she practices for choir. Her voice is beautiful and it is clear how much she loves to sing. It makes her happy, and that expands into other parts of her life. The performance isn't really the point.

I cannot tell you that rediscovering my love for writing helped me to find a job. But as I said, PLANS is not about cause and effect. It's about rebuilding yourself knowing that by focusing on these five areas of your life, everything else will follow. I am certain of this.

So, whatever it is that brings you joy, it's time to rediscover it now. Unemployment is a great experience for shining a light on your life but you don't have to be unemployed to implement PLANS or to find out what brings you joy. Bringing your passion back into your life will bring a happiness that you may not have seen since childhood. It will help bring balance and have a positive effect on other areas of your life.

With my passion fully rediscovered, I was already turning my attention away from the doom and gloom of being fired. Writing was bringing me joy and providing the distraction I needed. Able to look outwards once more, it was time to focus on the others in my life, my Loved Ones.

KEY LESSONS FROM CHAPTER 6:

- Rediscovering a passion you have long forgotten will lift your spirits and bring joy back into your life. This will be much needed and appreciated when you have been fired.

- Passions also serve the secondary purpose of making you memorable. This is particularly helpful when looking for a new job as it helps you stand out as a potential employee.

- If you don't have a passion from your childhood to reignite, then it's time to find one! Such is the popularity of passions in our modern age, all types of classes and activities have surfaced and are freely available to all.

CHAPTER 7:
L IS FOR LOVED ONES

Hard times will always reveal true friends.

Unknown

I am very fortunate to be part of a tight-knit group of friends that span school years, university years, London years and now marriage and baby years. The wonderful thing about having a tight friendship group is that people genuinely care about your well-being. The downside? People genuinely care about your well-being! You can't really hide from anything. These people love you and force you to face the reality of what is happening in your life. There is no chance of hiding behind false truths. They will see straight through the lies you tell yourself.

In April 2014 I flew home to New Zealand for the wedding of one of my closest friends and whilst excited, the idea of admitting to the truth filled me with dread. It had been four months and I was still unemployed, having missed out on jobs all over town. Facing myself was hard enough but flying home a complete failure was worse. Feeling like you have somehow let down the people you love is the toughest part of being fired.

THE THINGS WE DO FOR THE ONES WE LOVE

When it comes to making PLANS, especially when you are unemployed, Loved Ones is a very important pillar. Being unemployed is tough but trust me, it's equally as tough on the people around you. This is true of any difficult situation. When you are suffering it affects everyone you love.

The fiancé of a close friend had started his career in London in 2005 as a high-flying marketing director. Within a year he was lured by the money on offer in the City and took an entry-level role in finance. Despite a complete lack of experience he was still making £25k per year more than in his previous role. He enjoyed the high life of the City for two years before the Global Financial Crisis hit. Overnight, everything changed.

In 2005 the City was a place where no matter what qualifications you held you could pick up some sort of job that would inevitably pay more than anywhere else. But by the end of 2008 everything had changed. Every day the front pages of the big British newspapers reported another financial institution making extreme job cuts and there were redundancies all over town. Often the same institutions made repeat announcements just weeks after letting a cohort of workers go. It was constant. Understandably, those with little experience were some of the first to go.

Unemployed and unable to go back to marketing after a two-year hiatus, my friend spent the next nine months pondering his future. In the end he decided a move home to New Zealand was the best option. London no longer held the wealth and prosperity that so many Kiwis had originally moved for and like so many other New Zealanders the financial crisis was the catalyst for change.

Before he left, he did everything he could to get another job in London. But in 2008/09 the opportunities simply weren't out there. I would see his fiancé every few weeks during this time and the strain was considerable; it was etched all over her face. Being the sole provider of income was stressful but the emotional stress was harder. She was supporting them both. He lost his confidence and felt his 'manhood' was compromised by his fiancé providing for them. These emotions manifested themselves in anger most of the time. They were fighting a lot and there were times I wondered if we would ever see the day they walked down the aisle.

I'm happy to say we did. They married in 2010, less than a year after moving home. When she talks about his unemployment she reflects rationally. It was one of the most difficult times they have ever endured as a couple but as she says, 'There are much worse things we could have suffered together'.

Whilst enduring the crisis that follows being fired, it's important to recognise that you are not alone in this situation. Even if it doesn't feel like it at the time there is a whole team of people (your loved ones) who are selflessly supporting you all the way along. It's important to recognise and appreciate the support these people are giving you.

My friends are not alone. Losing your job when you are part of a couple is always very difficult for the partner. If there are children involved as well the strain is increased. But the people you love are the people who will see you through it. Whether it's unemployment or another difficult situation, making sure that your loved ones remain a key focus in your life is so important. It's easy to take their love and patience for granted.

MAKE THE ONES YOU LOVE, YOUR NUMBER ONE GOAL

Loved Ones is an area of my life I didn't nurture enough when I was unemployed. I knew that my situation was impacting those around me but I didn't really know how to stop it. I was miserable, and not that much fun to be around. The fact that I knew this made it even harder. I would act out of character but then instantly regret behaving in such a way. Only then would I get angry with myself for being so unbearable to be around and cut myself off more from people so to shelter them from my intolerable behaviour.

So I include Loved Ones as part of my PLANS more as reflection than practice. Now my friends and family form a significant part of my PLANS and I only wish I had put some of these practices in place earlier. If I had made my loved ones more of a focus, and consciously taken steps to include them in my life I may have been a nicer person to be around. Believe it or not, it is possible for your relationships to blossom in times like this. As it was the love and support I did receive during this time was more by default than by design. I am just lucky the people I love were willing to persevere with me even when times were tough.

In Chapter 6, I mentioned Lindsay Hopkins, the successful businessman and property investor I had the pleasure of meeting last year. It was Lindsay who really helped propel my thinking about planning and PLANS. Not only were his plans incredibly comprehensive, they included a huge element of Loved Ones. He had committed in his plan regular dates nights with his wife, a vow to drive three hours every month to visit his sister plus regular phone calls with other family members and time spent with his children.

At first it struck me as odd to include 'goals' around the people you love. Surely there was something disingenuous about setting a goal to ensure a connection with your family and friends? Very quickly I changed my mind. It makes complete sense that if we set goals in order to achieve great success in business and career, it is wise to apply the same level of planning to our personal relationships. Lindsay's goals were not lofty goals. It is not hard to pick up the phone every week and make a call. But the point was that if they were not included in his goals alongside everything else they would not get the same level of focus. And whilst easy to do, they were just as easy to bypass in favour of something more pressing. Without focus, our Loved Ones very quickly take a back seat to everything else we are trying to achieve.

Inspired by Lindsay, I decided in 2016 to make Loved Ones a serious focus in my goals for the year. One area of my personal life where I've always struggled is keeping in touch my younger brothers. Despite the ten to 13-year age gap between us we have always been close. So love and closeness is not an issue; it's more the 11,000 miles and the 12-hour time difference that I struggled with. Finding a time to call them is always tough when there are only really a couple of opportunities a week.

Despite the challenges, I decided to set a goal to ring my brothers once a month. It's not crazy ambitious but by putting it in my plan, it became a focus. It's right there in my 2016 goals on the same level of importance as investing in property and writing this book. If anything this goal is arguably more important than the other ones, because it involves two people I love.

By writing it down and committing to it I found I was forced to focus on how to make this happen every month. I soon realised that I had more opportunities to call them than I thought. In the morning on the bus between the gym and the office I have a 15-minute window to make phone calls. They are boys in their twenties so they don't want to talk to anyone on the phone for more than a quarter of an hour. This liberating realisation showed me that when you write something down and focus on it you discover ways to make it work.

Unfortunately I have failed to in my mission to speak to them every month. Despite my frequent calls, my youngest brother very rarely has his phone on him. The older one, however, answers pretty much every time. We chat for only 15 minutes but it starts my day off in such a great way that I know it is something I will continue to do. And despite the fact he never answers his phone, I know my youngest brother appreciates my efforts to speak. I think just seeing the missed call notification is bringing us closer together!

Writing goals that include your loved ones is the simplest yet most impactful area of PLANS. Whether it's committing to a weekly date night with your partner, a monthly dinner with your siblings or a daily phone call to your Mum, writing it down and making it a focus will see you achieve it.

THE TOUGH TIMES SHOW OUR TRUE COLOURS

I saw this simplicity at play a few years ago when a friend of mine was struggling in her marriage. She and her husband were fighting more than usual and it had become clear they were taking each other for granted more than ever before. Not wanting to end up another divorce statistic, my friend decided to set the goal of showing gratitude in her relationship every day. After reading a book that advocated this practice she set the goal to write in a journal every day one thing that she was grateful to her husband for. The goal was to have a complete journal by the end of the year that she could give to her husband as a Christmas present.

At first she found it difficult because they were fighting so often. However, as time went on, she found that the practice of forcing herself to think of one thing to appreciate every day actually saw her attitude towards their marriage start to change. With it her behaviour altered and before she knew it they were fighting less. She told me that because the things she loved about him were front of mind every day, she just couldn't complain or be frustrated with him about the small stuff any more.

If you don't commit to focusing on your loved ones already, losing your job will definitely make you see things differently. It's important to appreciate the toll your unemployment will have on the people around you. You are not alone in this experience, even though it really does feel like it most of the time. If you focus on your loved ones, and make them a priority, instead of just focusing on the immediate tasks like finding a new job you will be surprised how quickly your relationships transform and grow. Tough times are in fact an amazing time for discovering which people in your life really care about you.

Despite the fact I felt like I was constantly pushing people away the people that really cared about me were there all along. But this won't always be the case. If you don't understand the impact you are having on your loved ones when you are unemployed you may find yourself without the love and support you need to get through this time. You may not realise it but you are probably being a nightmare! You have definitely changed personality in some way, like over-compensating for bad behaviour like I did, or pushing people away due to the shame. And no doubt your confidence has tanked which is understandable when you have lost one of the key ingredients of your identity.

Showing your appreciation for your loved ones is the key to ensuring you come out the other end of the experience in a better position than the one you started in. So it is important to make them a focus. Set the goal: move your focus towards your loved ones and away from what is wrong. It will help you to remember how great the people in your life are and this gratitude will make it easier for you to remember to acknowledge those that love you.

If you are like me, you are lucky to be surrounded not just by an amazing group of friends but an amazing family as well. Through all the highs and lows of unemployment, they will be there in some way cheering you on. You might miss a lot of it at the time – it's hard, you've got so much to deal with - but trust me, it's there.

Almost eight months to the day after I was fired for the second time I arrived home to my apartment in London to find a box outside my door. It was the end of my first week back working in a permanent job. It was the happiest I'd been in a long time. I opened the box to find an orchid inside, growing beautifully in a ceramic pot. Next to the orchid was a card from my best friend and her fiancé in Sydney. On the card was written just two words: 'Welcome back'.

KEY LESSONS FROM CHAPTER 7:

- Being fired is tough not just on yourself but also on the ones you love. It is important to recognise the love and support they give you, even if it is hard to do at the time.

- Make your loved ones your priority by 'scheduling' them in your life the same way you schedule all the other important tasks. Don't let being busy or stressed mean that you forget to acknowledge the support they are giving you.

- Tough times show the true colours of those around us. It is possible for relationships to flourish and strengthen when you are struggling, as the people who really love you will stick by you through it all.

CHAPTER 8:
A IS FOR ACTIVITY

Wake up, work out, kick ass, repeat!

Unknown

There is huge amount of research and literature concerned with the benefits of keeping fit and healthy. But this is not a health book. I'm not going to recite all the reasons you should put down that doughnut and get your trainers on. We all know that good health and fitness are imperative to ensuring we live long, disease-free lives but there are many other reasons that fitness, or 'Activity' as we are calling it here is beneficial to our lives.

When I woke up in January 2014 as an unemployed bum my routine went out the window. I no longer had any place to be and despite my best efforts my day no longer had any sort of structure. I could sleep until lunchtime, stay up all night, watch movies at 3am; it really didn't matter.

The problem with this lack of structure is that's it's a very slippery slope. A slippery slope out of mainstream society and the world you hope to get a job back in. Once you start to withdraw from the everyday world it's hard to keep in touch.

The other problem you find is that you no longer face any sort of challenges in your day. If you are lucky your job and career keep you challenged and motivated. But when you lose your job, so much of that is gone.

My morning gym routine is the most consistently challenging activity in my life. I have always been an active person. I grew up in New Zealand, a country known for its outdoor lifestyle, so it's fairly impossible to avoid. As such, incorporating some sort of activity into my life is as natural for me as eating and sleeping. During that extended period of unemployment my morning gym routine gave me the motivation that being fired had taken away. Not only that, it's also meditative. Every morning I walk out of the gym feeling relaxed and frankly, a little bit high. It's incredible. So when my alarm goes off at 6am I don't associate going to the gym with a struggle. I associate it with meditation, calm and euphoria. But if a daily gym marathon is not your thing then that's okay there are plenty of other options!

JUST GET UP AND MOVE!

A is for Activity, not Health and Fitness, because (aside from the fact that Health starts with an H) the exciting revelation of this chapter is that one simple activity, not a regular gym session, is enough to keep you motivated and challenged. You do not need to be getting up at 6am and running 10km before breakfast. Nor do you have to be in the gym pushing weights. All you need to do is pick an activity that gets your heart rate up and commit to it on a regular basis.

For me during my never-ending job hunt it was my boot camp class at the gym. I took great comfort in continuing my routine of rising at 6am and taking part in my boot camp class. Not only did it make me feel like I was still part of the world it gave me the opportunity to really push my fitness levels. Every day I approached my class with the same intensity and focus I had once given my job and the results were incredible. I ran speeds on the treadmill I'd never seen before and discovered muscles on my stomach I never knew existed. Unemployment was definitely good for my fitness if nothing else.

However, despite the success of the boot camp, there was a different activity that I really credit with keeping my sanity during those long months. One morning not long after I'd been fired I emerged from the basement of my gym to discover London had woken to three-degree weather and a beautiful blue-sky day. There was literally not a cloud in the sky. As I had nowhere to be I decided to grab a coffee from the café next door and take the one hour walk through Kings Cross St Pancras, on to the canal at Islington and back to where I lived.

I'd never really understood the concept of 'walking'. Walking for me was something I did to get from A to B, but never a planned activity to derive pleasure in any way. I had heard of people who 'walked' for no apparent reason but it didn't make sense to me. My parents used to go for walks after dinner and I always thought it was an activity that people took part in once their body could no longer handle the intensity of running.

But the first morning I walked home along the canal, my spirit was lifted like it hadn't been lifted in a long time. I felt happy. My mind was calm. I noticed things I'd never seen before. An old boat café selling cups of tea and scones; a secret staircase up the side of the canal; the weird way that ducks and pigeons seemed to connect. By the time I got home I was floating. It was the best I'd felt in a month.

I remember once reading a list on one of those completely irrelevant websites that infiltrate your Facebook newsfeed. It was a list of advice to a 20-something, full of the usual cliché guidance people over 30 love to give folks ten years younger than them. But in amongst all the cheesy quotes there was one really awesome piece of advice that I had never seen on lists like this before. It said:

If you're feeling depressed and you're not sure why, there's an 80% chance you just need to leave your apartment and go for a walk!

It was not until I'd been walking regularly for about a month that I remembered this quote. Winter was dark and cold, but on the days when I woke up feeling sad (and that was often) getting out of the house and going for a walk put the sadness at bay, even if just for a short time. As long as you have two legs, you can walk. It requires very little skill, but done with purpose or for enjoyment can provide a huge number of benefits.

The Sunday Times recently ran an article about the benefits of walking. In it, they featured an interview with the writer Polly Vernon who, as it transpires, has had a 17-year love affair with walking. In the interview, Vernon described how walking is central to her wellbeing. She goes on to describe walking as 'meditative, it is endorphin-releasing. It reconnects you with the physical world you inhabit'. Reading this article reminded me of the love affair I had with walking. It is no longer a regular feature of my life. Sadly I don't have the time anymore (time is something you take for granted when you are unemployed). The lesson has stayed with me though: activity is the key to your mental well-being and walking is a great place to start.

RUN FORREST....

The other common activity that people commit to when they need challenge and focus is running. It feels boring and mainstream these days as every person I know seems to be a runner but there is a reason for that. In adult life unlike our childhood there are very few real opportunities to compete against yourself and others. As children we have school sport days, cross-country runs, spelling bees and exams. So many chances to test our skills. But as adults, outside of work, opportunities are limited. Running, like walking, generally does not require a lot of skill. But it certainly provides a mental battle.

In 2009 a close friend of mine was made redundant as part of a company restructure. Whilst her job was made redundant, she had the opportunity to apply for other jobs within the company. The process for redundancy and subsequent re-hire took four months. If being fired is a tough place to be being in this sort of limbo is equally difficult. Not knowing whether she would have a job in four months' time and under the daily pressure to perform to secure a new job, my friend turned to running as an escape.

Having never run a day in her life, she was inspired by the everyday people who take part in running events in the UK and decided to sign up to take part in the Great North Run, a half marathon in Newcastle. Ambitious though it is to run a half marathon, having never been a runner made the accomplishment even more spectacular. For three months, she rose at 6am and committed to the miles she had written down on her training schedule. When I asked her where this motivation had come from, her response was surprising for someone who had never been a runner. 'There is no need for motivation. I get up every day because it's the best part of my day. It's the only thing I do that isn't seeped in stress and anxiety. It calms my mind. Its keeps me focused. And it makes me feel like a winner. Why would I not get out of bed for this?' You can't argue with that!

The best thing about walking and running as your Activity is that they're relatively low-cost and it gets you out of the house in the fresh air. There is nothing more uplifting than this. However, if you do have the money, yoga is another activity that many people I know who have lost their jobs will advocate.

NAMASTE, MY FRIEND

For years, yoga was considered a niche activity, confined to people who grew organic vegetables, took retreats to India and ate vegan food. Perhaps it's less that yoga has become mainstream, and more that we seem to have all adopted some form of this lifestyle, with many of my acquaintances now advocating organic vegan diets and healing trips to India. Either way, as yoga has reached the masses it's easy to find a studio in most parts of the western world.

The popularity of yoga has been in part due to its ability to relax the body and calm the mind. As our lives have become more hectic and stressful, people have searched for different ways to counterbalance this and the activity of yoga is a consistent success story. I have many friends who credit yoga with reducing or eliminating all sorts of ailments, including anxiety and stress. One friend who practices yoga five days a week insists the reason she can fall asleep at night in under a minute is the result of yoga.

From my own experience, I can say that there is definitely a calming effect that comes with being in a yoga studio. I always arrive 15 minutes before the class is due to begin so that I can enjoy the extra time lying on the mat, slowing my breath and relaxing. Whilst I do not claim to have any talent whatsoever for yoga, the yoga studio is not a place for competition or judgement. No matter how tough the pose you are being asked to do, at any point you can relax back on your mat and chill out. No one cares. It is the least judgemental place in the entire world. Yoga is therefore a perfect Activity for your PLANS: a calming place where you can relax and let the stress of your unemployment drift away. A place where no one will judge you and no one will interrogate you. There is a reason Yogis are always so Zen.

In the end, it doesn't matter which activity you choose, the point is to get out there. Do something that challenges you. Get your heart rate pumping or just get your body moving. Find something that you enjoy and commit to making it a regular feature in your life, both during employment and unemployment. Whether high intensity heart-pumping or low impact meditative, Activity will keep you focused, keep you challenged and ultimately keep you sane. It may not directly help you find another job, but it will stop you from going completely crazy. No matter how small, regular activity is transformative. When you commit to adding and increasing activity in your life you commit to changing your life. You may never see the direct effect but trust me, it is there. Your self-esteem will rise and so will your confidence. If you have lost your job, there is nothing more important than this.

For my own personal journey with unemployment committing to activity everyday helped to keep me prepared for the job market too. I may have been unemployed but I looked fantastic. I had never been fitter or healthier. While the strain of unemployment was taking its toll mentally, I stopped it from showing physically. Activity was key to this, not just to ensure I looked sharp at job interviews, but so that all the new people I was meeting along the way were none the wiser about how I really felt inside. And that was very important because if I was going to find my dream job it wasn't going to come to me through an ad on LinkedIn. It was going to come through my network. Supported, passionate, fit and healthy, I was now ready to face the world!

KEY LESSONS FROM CHAPTER 8:

- Activity, whether strenuous or relaxing, is important to keep your mind focused. You don't need to be running a marathon but you do need to keep active. It will make you feel amazing and keep you looking good.

- Walking, running and yoga are three great activities that will not only keep you moving but also make you feel awesome.

- Choosing an activity that also has an added sense of achievement, for example running and then signing up to an organised run, will help build your confidence back.

CHAPTER 9:
N IS FOR NETWORK

You are the average of the five people you spend the most time with.

Jim Rohn

One of the big mistakes people often make when they are comfortable in their jobs and career is forgetting to keep in touch with their network. Even when people have succeeded in building a strong network within their organisation, they will often neglect to make contacts beyond the boundaries of work. Yet your external network is the more sustainable of the two. When you lose your job, it is scary how quickly your internal network can crumble.

Last year a close friend was made redundant from a company where he had worked for close to ten years. Yet when he was fired not a single person from the company – all his 'close' friends included – reached out to see if he was OK. People he had known most of his adult life were suddenly strangers. Even when he reached out to them personally, they expressed sympathetic condolence yet did not suggest their communication would extend beyond that phone call. He said it was an awakening he did not see coming. In fact, he found it even more shocking than the firing itself.

EXPANDING YOUR NETWORK

Building my network was the way I kept myself occupied during my second round of unemployment. Networking was an essential part of my PLANS, not only because it was the one thing that might directly find me a job but also because it got me out of the house and gave me human contact. It kept me in touch with the working world.

I've always been the type of person who loves to meet new people. I'm always interested to hear other people's stories and be inspired by where they have come from so I didn't find it hard to make meeting new people my number one task. Having said that, I've always hated the word 'networking'. It has such negative connotations and suggests a very disingenuous relationship between individuals. Of course, there will always be people who make contacts for individual gain but I naïvely like to think that in many networking situations people just love meeting other people.

As a result, I never really approached this part of my PLANS as 'networking'. I took the approach that I just wanted to meet loads of amazing people who could excite and inspire me as I moved into this next phase of my life. I knew that the best jobs in London weren't going to be advertised online or just fall in my lap, but I also knew that the journey was just as important as the destination. Hopefully, through all the new contacts I would make, a new job would somehow be the result. But it wasn't all about that. There was so much to be learned along the way from the many incredibly smart and talented people that I was lucky enough to meet.

It was important for me to take the opportunity to learn more about the possibilities open to me and not just focus on the next job. I had been working for the same company for eight years and wanted to hear more about the world outside. I wanted to open my mind to other industries, other careers, other ways of working and I was completely humbled by the responses to my request.

The key for me was to approach my friends and former colleagues in a way that they understood this wasn't just about finding a new job. I wanted to know about their careers, their lives, and their journey - where had they been, what had they done, what were their struggles. I approached people and invited them for coffee: not by telling them I was unemployed and looking for a job but by telling them I was looking for inspiration.

It's amazing how many people will meet you for coffee when you are interested in hearing about their life, instead of asking for a job. By approaching people and saying, 'you've obviously had a successful career, I'd love to hear more about it and get your advice on what you think I should do next', I was able to open up so many more doors than if I'd just been out networking focused on looking for a job.

The meetings were always informal in cafes or restaurants. It's easier to relax and connect with people when the setting is conducive to this. As such, people were always willing to share their stories with me. It inspired and motivated me and I always left these meetings feeling optimistic about the future.

But it was not one-sided. Most people I met with had an interest in my story as well. It helped to remind me that I had, in fact, had a very successful career: one that other people were also fascinated to hear about. That in itself helped to restore a great deal of my self confidence.

At the end of every meeting I would make sure to ask if they knew anyone they thought I should meet. Not someone who would be in a position to offer me a job, but someone who genuinely might be able to offer advice or thoughts that would keep pushing me in the right direction. All of my friends introduced me to new people; some of them three or four new people. Within in a week I had a new career as a professional coffee drinker. Some days I would meet as many as five new people. All of them were happy to introduce me to even more people. I based myself out of my favourite café in central London. If I wasn't meeting new contacts I was working on my job hunt and having friends drop in to keep me company. Very quickly I had gone from lonely and unemployed to holding down a 'full time job'.

EXPLORING NEW CAREERS

Every meeting that took place not only served the purpose of filling my days but inspired me to believe that I could pursue any career direction I wished. Hearing stories of people navigating their way through the ups and downs of their careers is a great antidote to your own woes.

It turned out my friends had worked all over the world, for all types of companies, in an amazing range of different fields, and they had plenty of great advice for the next move in my career. Once we got into the detail of where they had been and the circumstances with which they had moved from one job to the next, the juices of inspiration would start to flow.

One friend began his career working as an account manager in the creative studio of a large advertising agency (a very similar start in life as me) before moving successfully to become a management consultant. Another friend had studied art history at university, before moving into television advertising, quitting her job and then starting her own restaurant. I even met up with a friend who started his life in marketing alongside me and had recently quit to go to medical school!

During the first two months of my job hunt, I met with 26 people I already knew, and 33 people I had never met. Off the back of these 59 meetings I explored new career options that included studying to gain entry to a top tier business school; working for celebrity chef Gordon Ramsey; becoming a management consultant; retraining as a lawyer; writing a book (interesting!); going travelling (not really a career, but a very good option); working in a bar on a Caribbean Island (see 'going travelling'); and staring my own consultancy.

In the end, the job that ended my unemployment came through a recruiter. However the introduction to this obscure recruiter came through a business contact that introduced me to his old boss who introduced me to this recruiter. So as it turns out, my career as a professional coffee-drinker was incredibly lucrative.

UNLIKELY HEROES

The other important lesson I learnt is that you find heroes in unlikely places.

Before I was fired for the second time, I did a piece of brand strategy work which was pitched out to two different strategy agencies. Unfortunately, there can only be one winner in a pitch process. For the agency I turned down I did so with a heavy heart as I had a huge respect and warmth for their founder, Matt.

Matt is a very smart, well-respected guy who had a stellar advertising agency career that he transformed into a successful business career. His agency lost the pitch for no other reason than there were two competing agencies and I had to choose one. So you can imagine how much of a fool I felt when I called him up three months later to ask for his advice on the next steps of my career.

I felt pretty sheepish arriving at Matt's offices on a cold winter's morning. Although he had been quick to invite me to visit I couldn't help but feel as though I was somehow taking advantage of his goodwill. To my surprise, Matt not only opened up his thoughts on where I should head next in my career, he also opened up his phone and introduced me to six people right there on the spot! Before I left the office I had coffee dates with three of them. He also opened up his office and told me that I could work there whenever I was going stir-crazy at home and needed a place to go.

Matt will forever be one of the heroes of my unemployment - a top bloke, who was not only incredibly kind but perfectly positioned to offer me advice and guidance. Matt was also the person who started the chain of introductions which led me to the job that ended my unemployment.

Be willing to accept help when it is given and recognise when an unlikely hero might be right in front of you. You never know when the right connection will click that will lead you somewhere amazing. The key is to open your mind to the possibilities and just keep hustling for knowledge. There is never a bad coffee date when you are a full-time networker; every meeting is an opportunity to learn something new.

THE PERFECT REFERENCE

Extending your network after being fired is almost more important than when you are in employment because you really need people to know you well if you are going to get your new job. Telling a future employer that you were fired from your previous job is never an easy conversation to have. But if you are having it with someone who already knows you, or for whom you have been already validated through a mutual acquaintance, the conversation is less awkward. On paper being fired looks awful; people conjure up all sorts of negative images of what sort of person you must be. The reality, as we have already established, is that it happens to loads of incredibly talented and valuable employees.

I made a habit of seeking out jobs through my network. The more I grew my network, the more opportunities came my way. The trick was to ensure that when I sat down with a potential employer, I had already been recommended by someone. It took the edge off the unemployment blip on my CV, which suggested a cause for concern. Since other people had spoken to validate me I was able to rely more on my real abilities, rather than what was written on my CV. In the course of my seven months of job-hunting, not one interviewer spent more than 2 minutes delving into what had happened at the job from which I was fired;

some of them didn't even bring it up. Having your network speak on your behalf is absolutely priceless when you have lost your job.

Whether you have been fired or are still in employment, extending your network is the most valuable thing you can do for your career. For reasons of ease and comfort, many of us forget to keep a wide network of people when we are in secure jobs. We wait until we really need a network to build it up, but you never know how essential your external network might be one day There is also so much to be gained from a network over and above your next job; the people you surround yourself with help to stimulate you and keep you inspired. They open up ideas and ways of thinking that challenge the way you live your life.

Be social. Get out of the house and meet people (whether you are unemployed or not). Say 'yes' to invitations, even if you are tired and don't feel like going out. Ask strangers for coffee; reach out to old friends and colleagues; keep your social and professional networks alive. Don't contact people just for your own gain but know that in all relationships, there is always something you can learn. Over and above all else, we are human beings and human contact is what keeps us alive.

And that is why the final piece of our PLANS is Soul.

KEY LESSONS FROM CHAPTER 9:

- Networking does not have to be disingenuous. It's not about schmoozing for a new job but about meeting new people and being inspired by them.

- Networking is an opportunity to explore new careers and be encouraged by the experiences of others. You never know where a coffee meeting might take you!

- Your network provides the perfect reference for your future job. Having someone recommend or vouch for you, is the perfect way to avoid having to explain why you left your last job.

CHAPTER 10:
S IS FOR SOUL

Invent your world. Surround yourself with people, colours, sounds and work that nourish your soul.

Susan Ariel Rainbow Kennedy

When I was younger, I remember my parents had a book called 'Chicken Soup for the Soul'. The book was a series of inspirational stories that demonstrated the very best qualities of human beings – compassion, forgiveness, generosity and faith. It has since gone on to become a very famous book – indeed, a series of books – which has been published in 40 languages and sold more than 100 million copies in the US alone.

It's not difficult to understand why this book became so wildly successful. For generations, human beings have been inspired by the knowledge that there exists in all of us a higher level of emotional connection; that when we reach out and connect with other human beings there is a magic that can happen, having a euphoric effect on the individuals involved. Yet in the craziness of our modern-day existence very few people take the time to really connect with other human beings and use this unique power to enrich all of our lives.

Reading a book like 'Chicken Soup for the Soul' makes you feel good about the world. It lifts you up and inspires you to want to live a more fulfilled life. The problem is, for most people, the moment the book goes back on the shelf, the lessons we have learnt are forgotten. We love the idea of nourishing our soul and the souls of others, but we never really get round to doing it.

NO BETTER WAY TO LIFT YOURSELF UP

'S' is for Soul, because there is no better way to lift yourself from the fog of unemployment than by making a plan that includes nourishing your soul by connecting with other human beings. Stop being the person that only focuses on their own problems and instead find ways to connect with people on a level that you never did in your pre-unemployment life.

As human beings, we focus the majority of our attention on ourselves. When you look at a photo of a group of people, the first person you seek out is yourself. When a conversation is taking place close by, you don't hear any of it until your name is mentioned. When you read a tragic global news story, you feel sad but think first about how it might affect you. We are wired to think of ourselves first. It's how we survive.

When you are fired from a job suddenly the whole world is about you. As you change into survival mode, you start to miss everything else that is going on around you and instead think only of yourself. You look at other people – those with jobs – and feel jealous that they have somewhere to go every day. You feel frustrated when friends complain about their daily lives wishing you had the same such trivial worries to complain about. The world feels overwhelming and it's hard to imagine anyone has problems but you.

Of course, the reality is quite the opposite; everyone else has their own problems too. Scratch the surface of someone's perfect life and you will find it is not as perfect as you imagined. This realisation should give you some comfort but it doesn't. Because lost in self-pity, you fail to see what's taking place in other people's lives.

The previous chapter should have given you some idea how rewarding and productive making contact with others can be during a low period of your life. If networking is about connecting with people to grow and nurture your professional life, Soul is about connecting with other human beings as a way of mutually enriching each other's lives. If you can lift yourself out of the fog for long enough to feel genuine compassion for the plight of other people you may find yourself being lifted further again. At the very least, you will find yourself inspired by the resilience, generosity and kindness other humans regularly display.

Connecting with others will not always be easy; unemployment challenges you in a way that feels overwhelming at times. At first, you will certainly feel that it is difficult to give any time or compassion to other people but trust me, the experience of human connection and compassion for others will put your unemployment in perspective like nothing else can.

A LESSON IN RESILIENCE

On 13th December 2013 when I found myself unemployed for the second time, I felt as if my whole world had caved in. All the plans I had for the next few years were suddenly gone. It felt as if my life was a disaster of epic proportions and that everyone should feel sorry for me.

Self-centred, I know. But unfortunately it is a feeling that comes all too easily when you have been fired. Thankfully, this feeling didn't last very long.

On 27th December, after a wonderful few days celebrating Christmas in Berlin, I arrived in Krakow, a city I had wanted to visit since I was a teenager. My first day in Krakow was a stunning blue-sky day. I walked the city in the sunshine, drinking mulled wine in the Christmas markets, feeding ducks on the riverbank and eating Polish stew. It was an amazing and uplifting day. For anyone who has travelled, you will know that very little nourishes the soul the same way travelling does.

But it wasn't Day One in Krakow that made me re-evaluate the real disaster of my unemployment. It was Day Two.

For years I had wanted to visit Auschwitz. I loved World War Two history when I was at high school in New Zealand, but the distance to Europe always made it feel more like a story, than something that actually happened. So on Day Two of my trip to Krakow, I visited the world's most famous concentration camp; the place where it is estimated over a million people, mainly Jews, died during the Holocaust.

Believe me when I tell you, there is nothing more powerful than a tour of Auschwitz to snap you out of self-pity and misery. If you want to feel the true insignificance of your problems, stand next to the crumbling concrete remains of a crematorium once used to gas over a million human bodies and see if you still feel the weight of the world on your shoulders.

I remember our guide telling a story about one of the few people to have escaped from Auschwitz. Upon realising that people were being gassed in a crematorium near the forest – something very few people realised until it was too late – this man knew he had to find a way out. He found a truck that was heading to mass graves outside of Auschwitz and laid himself on top of dead bodies. Through the stench of the corpses, he played dead until they arrived at the gravesite. Thrown into the mass grave and covered in dead bodies, he lay still and lifeless until he knew the Nazi soldiers had gone and he could escape. He was one of very few prisoners to escape the concentration camp.

The lesson I took from this story, and the countless stories of other prisoners who endured the most inhuman conditions and treatment, was to question my own resilience. How is it possible for human beings to be faced with such unfathomable horror and survive to tell the story? If I found myself faced with a similar situation, would I find the same strength? Do I have this sort of resilience in me or would I crumble?

And so I reflected on my own situation at the time. Unemployed, yes. But fit and healthy, with a wonderful family and friends, savings in the bank and a formerly successful career from which to launch my new one. Was life really that bad?

Now I understand there is a massive gulf between living in Nazi Germany and living in modern-day Britain. But putting your problems in perspective is an important part of moving forward post-unemployment, or let's be fair, even in our employed lives. The realisation that human beings had survived a lot worse than losing their job was a very blunt reminder that I could not dwell on my situation forever.

But you don't have to travel the world and experience the tragedies of history to witness the strength of the human race. All around you there are opportunities to nourish your soul through connecting with other people. For my part, the experience of Auschwitz inspired me to stop looking at my situation with such self-pity and come back in the New Year with a renewed sense of optimism and the beginnings of a plan. Don't get me wrong; I wasn't positive every day, but the perspective I took from my experience of Auschwitz was immeasurable.

CONNECTING HUMANITY

Soul isn't just about taking lessons from the resilience of others; it's about experiencing the inner satisfaction of opening up to other humans wherever you go. Whether you volunteer at a soup kitchen, teach sport to under-privileged children, or simply commit to ring the old lady next door to say goodnight each day, the renewed sense of happiness you will feel through giving and connecting with others will be immense. You will soon start to see your own situation with fresh eyes and once you have stepped out of the self-pity and put unemployment into perspective, you will be ready to start building an amazing new life.

So how do you build this into your PLANS? It's really about finding a way to connect with other human beings that makes you feel happy and good about the world.

Travelling is an easy one. People travel for many different reasons but the connection you feel with people from different backgrounds and ethnic diversities nourishes the soul in a deep and meaningful way. A close friend of mine once spent five months travelling through Africa. Late one afternoon she had left her tour group and was walking along the beach when she came across a young girl playing in the sand. The girl was very excited to see a foreign face and my friend found the girl endearing. Neither one spoke the other's language but they managed to connect with each other through smiles and mime. After half an hour the girl motioned to my friend to come with her towards her village not far from the beach. The wary Western traveller was apprehensive, but the compassionate human being was excited and intrigued, so she followed the young girl back to the village.

When they arrived at the village, the girl excitedly introduced my friend to everyone she could find. Even though she had no idea what was being said, my friend later told me she had never felt so much love and warmth from strangers. When they reached the girl's home she went about preparing a drink for my friend. As she looked at the murky water that was being used to prepare the drink, my friend was positive that if she drank the drink she'd be ill for days. It certainly went against all health warnings she had received upon arrival in Africa. But she drank it anyway, such was the strength of the connection she had made with the young girl.

Travel is good for the soul. It connects us with people we would not meet in our everyday life and reminds us of the power of human emotions. If you are unemployed, travel will not necessarily be an option but I challenge you to adopt the philanthropy of travel and apply it to your life. Connect with people that you would not usually meet; volunteer to help others; show compassion and empathy for those around you. Every day attempt to add happiness to other people's lives.

While it's been three years since I was fired for the second time, the lessons I learnt and the plans I built have made my life post-unemployment more rewarding and fulfilling than I could have ever imagined. Soul has been a big part of that. I've built charity and volunteering into my yearly plans and have taken the time to help and connect with others. In the past my busy life would not have allowed that to happen.

BEING AN INSPIRATION FOR OTHERS

During that time, I also realised it's possible to inspire and motivate other people just through being positive and showing them their own self-worth. And that through doing this you will nourish your own soul as well as theirs.

I was reminded of this recently on a trip to the town where I have my property business. I was coming to the end of a busy Saturday of viewings and I had just one house left to view. As we property investors do, I asked the vendor – an attractive middle-aged woman – why she was selling the house. It transpired she had split from her husband and the house was collateral damage. I instantly felt guilty for asking too much but she forged on, telling me her story.

What unfolded was the beautiful story of a woman, born in a generation who were told they were not supposed to add more value to the world other than to be mothers and wives. She had lost a newborn child to cot death and not long after losing her child, she had lost her mother. Her marriage had ended and she had remarried, only to find that this marriage was not as she had expected. She was often alone whilst her husband spent weekends at the pub with his friends. In the end she found the strength to leave him.

Instantly I felt a connection with this woman. We could not have possibly been from more different backgrounds but there was something about her I really liked. She was in her 50s, had been married for 20 or so years and found herself on her own for the first time since she was a teenager. She told me that she had never been on a 'girls' holiday', never had nights out without her husband, never thought her role in life was to do anything other than serve the man she married.

The viewing was scheduled for 15 minutes; I stayed for an hour. We chatted and bonded. She told me stories from her life that broke my heart and I felt like I wanted to inspire her to seize this new opportunity she had. I took her number and promised to meet up again next time I was up in the area. Later that evening she sent me a text. It said,

> 'Listening to you today made me realise life is for living. I found a new strength. So thank you'.

Words from a total stranger and I have never felt so moved.

My advice as you build your PLANS for your new life is to make Soul something that you don't just do on trips abroad but something you do every day. Take the time to slow down and look at the people around you. Find strength in their struggles and help them if you can. Connect with strangers. Talk to your taxi driver. Hear his story. Smile at the checkout clerk and ask how their day is going. Spread happiness and joy wherever you go. It will put your own life in perspective and it will nourish your soul. And you just never know when you might be nourishing the soul of others, too!

KEY LESSONS FROM CHAPTER 10:

- Connecting with people around us – friends, family and strangers alike – can lift your spirit in a way that little else can.
- Taking the time to hear the stories of others, especially those who have experienced great tragedy and struggle, can put your own problems in perspective and provide a true lesson in resilience.
- Soul is not just about being inspired by others, but also about inspiring them. Giving to others through your own strength will mutually enrich your lives.

PART III: REBUILDING YOUR LIFE

CHAPTER 11:
A NEW LIFE WITH STRUCTURE

Our daily rituals don't just set the tone of our day; they can also make us happier, more productive, and more successful.

———————————————————————————————— **Ilya Pozin**

So, now that you're on the path to perfecting your PLANS, life should just all fall back into place shouldn't it? Well, not quite. Making PLANS after being fired is the best thing you can do for yourself and those around you but it's just the first part of the puzzle. Supporting your plans with the right structure and mind set is important to make sure you get the most out of what you've set into motion.

One of the interesting things about unemployment is that although you may actually have less demand on your time, it's easy to feel more frantic when two or three things show up in your day. If you are serious about implementing your PLANS, then there will suddenly be more than that to contend with. Having no structure can leave you feeling like your life is out of control.

It is important to create a structure to your days that supports your PLANS, not only to ensure you get everything done, but also to keep you functioning as if you're still part of the mainstream world. Having your PLANS in place will ensure you remain healthy and motivated, which is essential if you are going to stay on top of your game. When the opportunity arises to snag the job of your dreams, you need to make sure you have the appearance – both physically and mentally – of someone that has their life together. Losing motivation and not looking after yourself can very quickly manifest in a physical signal to future employers that perhaps you aren't as desirable as someone who is currently employed. You need to have the right mind set if you are going to create an amazing new life.

CREATE A FOCUS, AND ACT!

Structure is incredibly important. It's a key part of what keeps you motivated. You need to synchronise with the rest of the world or you will fall out of society and it does not take long!

At the start of my own unemployment, I watched a ton of Netflix. As the weeks went on it became hard to distinguish between a Saturday and a Thursday. I lost track of the working week and started to feel cut off from my friends. I remember one particular Tuesday after my return from Poland. It was early January and probably one of the first days back at work for the rest of the world's population. I woke late, caught up on some emails from the comfort of my bed and thought long and hard about what I'd do that day. I decided my biggest achievement was going to be a long walk through Victoria Park, rugged up and enjoying the cold winter's air. I was actually really looking forward to it. However, before I went walking, I was going to tap into my daily Netflix fix.

Inspired by my experience of Krakow, I decided to finally watch Schindler's List, 20 years after the rest of the world. Now granted, Schindler's List is a very long movie, just over three hours to be exact. I knew this when I put it on. Yet I was still shocked when the January sun started to fade from my bedroom window and I realised the day (or at least the daylight) was over. How on earth did I manage to lose an entire day of my life?! Disappointed I'd missed the opportunity to walk around the park in what had been a cold but beautifully sunny day, it was then I realised the importance of keeping a structure. Unemployment may mean no job, but it does not have to mean you let your days drift away.

So back I went to my old routine – minus the job. My alarm would go off at 6am, I would be in the gym at 7am, work out for an hour, grab a coffee and then walk home along the canal (my new Activity). By the time I got home my motivation was high. I was feeling alive from my workout and relaxed from my walk. I'd cook up a healthy breakfast – kale and eggs had become my standard! – then jump online to start my day from the desk in my living room. It wasn't a bustling office but in my head it was the place I got down to work. If I wasn't working from home, I was working from various cafés in central London, moving from meeting to meeting. I liked to pretend that I was part of the London freelance scene that frequent central London cafés, instead of an unemployed bum trying to keep control of my sanity.

I kept to this routine every day; it was my new 'job'. I had meetings in my diary. Even if they were coffee meetings with friends, I scheduled them like I was the CEO. I had work to do in between replying to emails, re-writing my CV, following up on meetings. I was busy. I may not have been paid but I was working!

YOU WILL LEARN TO LOVE STRUCTURE

Whatever your situation is, make sure you keep a structure. Surprisingly, you will find that the structure is something you will love about unemployment. By keeping a structure, you keep a sense of your old life. As weird as it may sound, there will be a joy you will get from connecting with your old life whilst building a new one. You are less likely to feel lost.

Everyone's situation is different. For me, it was important to keep getting out of bed at 6am. This was naturally much harder to do knowing I didn't have anywhere to be during the day, but by locking in a boot camp session, paying for it and committing to it, I was able to keep my sanity and appear as if I was still going places.

It's not necessary to keep the same structure you had before. You may decide that unemployment presents the perfect chance to create a new one that works better for you. Maybe you have been the frantic working parent who never had time to pick up the kids from school. Now your new routine could involve making lunches in the morning, and dropping kids off at sports practice. Or perhaps you are really a night owl who gets their best work done after 10pm. Change your routine. You don't need to keep to 9-5 hours; do whatever works best for you.

The main point is that you keep some sort of structure going so you get things done during your day. The motivation and self-esteem that comes from achieving something is worth it in itself! Don't binge on Netflix and sleep away your life; with your PLANS in place there is no excuse for running out of things to fill your days. Hopefully you are busy delving into your Passion, plus your Activity and Networking will give you plenty to do. In amongst all that, you'll be making time for your Loved Ones and connecting with others as you nourish your Soul. Build a structure around these five areas of your life and you'll be racing towards an amazing new world.

> **For a detailed breakdown of my daily routine during my unemployment go to www.LifeAfterFired.com to request a copy.**

That's the thing about unemployment, the blueprint for your life has gone and it's too easy to let things fall apart. But this is actually the perfect opportunity to create something new. Whatever it may be is totally up to you. Take the chance to create a new structure in your life, and make it the first step on the way to creating a whole new world. One you love and can't wait to be living.

BE THE DESIGNER OF YOUR LIFE

If you are enjoying the sound of this, you may be wondering if you would ever want to give it up when a job comes your way. But actually, designing the structure of your unemployment is your practice run for designing the shape and size of your future working life. When you come out the other side, you are still in a position to dictate the structure of your new life. Even if society tells you that you must work within a 9-5 vacuum, let the most important lesson of your unemployment be that you can actually create anything you want.

My close friend Sarah is a shining example of this. Not long after I found work after being fired for the second time, Sarah was fired from her job. Without any encouragement, Sarah went straight out and created a fabulous new life. She kept the structure in her days and when she finally did go back to working, it was on her terms.

Instead of going back to five days a week, she negotiated four-day weeks into any job she took. Flicking between freelance roles, she was unrelenting in this one detail. When asked by a new colleague what she did on Fridays, Sarah responded 'I do yoga at 9am and I have lunch with friends, and then I potter around Portobello market.' 'Oh, so you don't have children then?' said the new colleague. 'No', she responded, 'you don't need children to take Friday off. It's just the life I chose to live.'

Remember, being fired has thrown your life up in the air. Whatever comes back down and the formation it chooses to fall in is entirely up to you. There are no rules. Create your new life. Test out different structures to see what works best for you. Incorporating your PLANS will already make your life somewhat different to the life you started with, so your structure will naturally change as well. Your new structure will support your PLANS as well as supporting your new life, with the added bonus of helping to keep you sane!

The ease of your life flowing within a structure will ensure you keep calm and relaxed. I know this from experience. I felt panicked and disappointed in myself the day I realised I had wasted the whole afternoon watching Schindler's List instead of engaging in my Activity. A walk around Victoria Park would have been so much better for my mental health than watching Netflix. In hindsight, I realised it was the lack of control over my day that caused me distress. I felt like I had lost control over my world completely.

Fast-forward two weeks from that day and it was my 32nd birthday. I woke at 6am and went to the gym, and then I spent the morning at a café in central London 'working', followed by an afternoon in the cinema watching a movie. This time the afternoon didn't feel wasted despite the fact it was essentially the same activity as I'd done 2 weeks earlier. It was the structure to my day that made it more acceptable. I'm not saying don't take the time to relax and watch movies, I'm saying plan it like you would when you are employed. This will make you feel so much more in control of your life and ultimately happier. That's the funny thing about structure; it sounds like something that keeps you chained up but in fact it is the most liberating thing you can do for yourself at this time.

KEY LESSONS FROM CHAPTER 11:

- Putting PLANS in place will not be successful unless it is accompanied by a structure. Having a structure will allow you to feel in control and ready to tackle the day, as well as helping you excel in your PLANS.

- Far from feeling like a constraint, you may be surprised to find that having a structure is the thing you love the most. It is in fact incredibly liberating due to the sense of control you feel.

- You don't need to keep the structure you had before you were fired; you can create any new structure you like. Let this experience be the first step in creating the life you want once you find a new job.

CHAPTER 12:
RULES FOR LIVING

The only time you should ever look back is to see how far you have come.

Unknown

Having PLANS and sticking to a structure were the cornerstones of my survival during my initial unemployment and subsequent job hunt. Had I not set out my five key areas of focus and maintained a structure in my day, I would have completely lost my way. Being fired and then facing the challenges of unemployment completely rocks your world; the only way to survive is to make sure you are still the one with your hands on the controls.

Despite feeling like I had a pretty good plan of attack for whatever unemployment threw at me, there was one more simple strategy I employed to keep me feeling like I was winning every day. Underlying my PLANS and my daily structure were three deceptively simple rules I made myself live by to keep my eye on the ball.

THE RULES

Now you will probably read these and think they don't sound like much! But that's the point. They were very simple and easy to remember. They didn't tax my brain but they got my blood pumping whenever I thought about them. Don't take these rules lightly; they may not look like much at first but they made all the difference on the days when I was struggling. These three simple rules were the difference between turning off my alarm and crawling back under the covers and getting out of bed and attacking the day.

Rule One: Don't look back

It's so easy in life to spend all our time looking in the rear-view mirror; human beings – especially women – love to obsess about what went wrong. Whether it's relationships, jobs or friendships, we love to look back and analyse why things didn't work out. Whether or not we admit it to ourselves, we're often looking for someone to blame or painting a rosy picture of a world that is no longer ours. Both of these are destructive and hold you back from where you want to go. Reminiscing won't get you anywhere. The best place in life isn't in what's already happened; it's actually right here in the present. Looking forward perhaps but never forgetting what's happening today.

I once read a quote that said, 'there are far better things in our futures, than we ever leave behind'. I don't know where I read it, but it stuck with me. You don't know what is around the corner but you have to believe, especially when you are unemployed, that something amazing is about to happen. Because it is. I know, I've been through this twice. There is a time in the not-so-distant future when you will look back on this experience and feel glad it's over but pleased you had it. Your future self will be so much more powerful for having persevered through difficult times.

I can safely say after I was fired from my second job that I wasted very little time thinking about my former boss or his company once I'd picked myself up off the floor. Of course I worried about what was going to happen next but I didn't waste any time trying to overanalyse what had happened. Once I had reframed the story in my head, I moved on as fast as possible and I advise you to do the same.

Rule Two: Don't feel sorry for yourself

The easiest way to keep living by this second rule was to ensure I had adequately reframed the situation in my mind. I didn't want to spend the following months wallowing in self-pity and obsessing over the challenging situation life had thrown at me. Feeling sorry for yourself drains a lot of energy. I tried it for the first few weeks but I soon realised that it's really not that much fun.

Reframing the situation, coupled with my trip to Poland, helped me to get over myself. At the beginning, I was obsessed with 'me' and how 'bad' my situation was. I couldn't see anything positive and even though I had a million things to be grateful for gratitude was hard to come by. Once I realised how draining it was to feel sorry for myself, I implemented my new rules for living and started to be thankful for the positive things in my life. Very quickly I began to see the unlimited opportunity life had thrown at me. For the first time I believed that maybe this was all going to be worth it.

I admit there were still plenty of times over the course of the following months when I really did throw my own little pity party. But committing to live by the rule of 'not feeling sorry for myself' definitely helped kick me out of this feeling of pity any time it crept up on me. Believing with deep conviction that I had been given an amazing opportunity is what stopped me from crying into my coffee for months on end.

Rule Three: Come Back Fighting

I had these three small words written on my wall in big bold letters. Life is always going to throw you curve balls; what matters is how you respond.

My favourite spectator sport is tennis. I have a huge respect and admiration for tennis players. It is one of the only sports in the world where the game is literally not over until someone wins match point. This means you can come back from any imaginable score to win a game. You just have to start by preventing your opponent from winning match point, then winning the game, then winning the set and so on. You can be down 6-0 6-0 6-6 and in a tie-break, and still come back to win. For this reason, I think tennis players are the ultimate fighters. If you can keep a winning mind set and really believe you will come back to win regardless of the score, you always can.

I remember watching the semi-final match between Serena Williams and Maria Sharapova at the 2005 Australian Open. In the time since this match, these two players have gone on to have a continuing fierce rivalry, usually dominated by Williams. However, at this early stage in their careers it was Sharapova who was the more dominant, having beaten Williams in the Wimbledon final the year before. So when Sharapova was in the lead with 6-2 5-4, you would have expected it to be a fairly straightforward victory. Not so, as Williams came back to win the next three games and take the second set. In the third set, Sharapova was again leading 5-4 but let three match points slip away. Three times, Williams was on the brink of losing the game and three times she came back. The ultimate fighter, she then went on to take the final set 8-6, advance to the final and win the Australian Open.

From that day it was forever etched in my mind that nothing is over until it really is over. Keep fighting. Keep swinging. Keep a winning mind set.

This is the thinking I applied to my job hunt. No matter how many jobs I missed out on or how low my confidence was from being fired. No matter how many people told me I wasn't qualified. I knew I would come back fighting and that I would 'win'.

A LESSON IN PERSEVERANCE

Don't look back; don't feel sorry for yourself; and come back fighting. These three simple ideas had a powerful impact on my ability to move forward after being fired. If 'winning' and success is all about mind set, these simple rules brought me back to the right frame of mind whenever the strain of unemployment pushed me off course. Repeating them in my head would pump me up and give me strength, even if I wasn't feeling particularly strong.

Having PLANS and a structure were crucial to helping get my life back on track. Without them I would have been lost at sea, trying to work out what to do next. But I needed my Rules for Living to keep me moving when things got tough. On days when I felt like giving up these three simple rules kept my head above water.

There were more days than I can possibly count when I woke up feeling like I was making no progress. Even if I was implementing my PLANS I often felt like nothing was moving. Every day from mid-January to March I stuck to my systems, followed my structured day and kept reaffirming the need to not feel sorry for myself. And every day during that time nothing happened. In March, when I managed to get some freelance work, I adjusted my routine but continued to pursue my PLANS and follow the rules. For three more months, nothing happened.

It took a full seven months of plugging away before I finally broke through and was offered two incredible jobs in the same week. It felt like an eternity. I had never been so committed to something in my life, nor so focused on achieving it. Yet for seven months I felt like I was never going to be permanently employed by anyone again. I was doing all the things I thought I was meant to do, but nothing was happening.

When I finally burst through the other side it was an incredible feeling of relief mixed with a strange sense of surprise that I had actually achieved what I set out to do. I didn't have much of a choice but to find a new job, but I felt as far away from that goal in month seven as I did month one. So much so that it came as an utter shock when two amazing jobs fell in my lap. Only those close to me could see the hard work and perseverance that went on behind the scenes to land these two jobs. To everyone else, I looked like the luckiest person on earth.

My perseverance had paid off. My PLANS helped me to grow, thrive and stay connected with the working world; my structure kept me sane, but it was my rules for living that kept me on track. The rules were the secret sauce that helped me stay positive as I stuck to my structure and persevered with the same tasks over and over again. This perseverance was worth it.

THE SLIGHT EDGE

In his book, *The Slight Edge*, Jeff Olson states that successful people achieve success, not through superior talent or good luck, but because they keep doing the same basic things over and over again. They don't give up, even if those tasks are boring or mundane (which they usually are), even if they don't feel like they are moving anywhere (which is exactly how I felt), and even if you can't see the way out at the end. Successful people wake up every day and keep pushing.

Then, when you least expect it, the momentum you have built will propel you forward to success. All the hard work that you thought the universe hadn't noticed will suddenly pay off.

It wasn't until two years after I lost my job for a second time that I read this book, but the concept of *The Slight Edge* is exactly the lesson I learnt in those seven months.

The part that got me to the new life and the new job was the fact that I kept doing these things over and over again, even though I continually felt like I wanted to give up. Giving up would have been leaving the UK and moving home to New Zealand. It wasn't something I wanted to do but it felt like the only option when I was struggling to find permanent work. What I didn't realise at the time was that the momentum I was creating by doing these same small activities time and again was moving me quickly towards my goal. I didn't see it until I knocked through the other side and came up clutching two amazing jobs in my hand! That's the concept of *The Slight Edge*.

There is a quote, often attributed to Albert Einstein, that says, 'the definition of insanity is doing the same thing over and over again but expecting different results'. That definitely felt true to me! I had always thought this was a great quote until my 'Slight Edge' experience taught me otherwise. It was quotes like this that had me questioning whether persevering with my same strategy for months on end was a sensible plan. It was definitely driving me insane, that's for sure! But the silent force working in the background was bringing me closer to success.

At the time, I felt like maybe I had got lucky in the end; that actually I had been doing the wrong things but that some goodwill in the universe saved me in the eleventh hour. It wasn't until I read *The Slight Edge* that I realised what was really at play. There are forces in ourselves that are greater and more powerful than we can imagine. We can mobilise them ourselves but they won't always be visible. We have to trust that if we continue to work hard and push in the right direction eventually we will crash through to the other side. And that when we arrive, life will be amazing.

That's why the rules are important. There will be days when you feel like you are making no progress whatsoever and you will want to give up. It will be difficult to comprehend that somewhere in the background an invisible force is moving you forward. But if you keep those rules in the back of your mind it will keep your head above water. My rules reminded me not to give up. They reminded me that until someone won match point, I was still in the game. Every time I got knocked back I picked myself up again because I refused to feel sorry for myself. While my PLANS and structure were being implemented daily, my rules were what pushed me to keep going. It was incredible to see that something so simple could have such a massive impact.

KEY LESSONS FROM CHAPTER 12:

- While PLANS and structure are crucial to help get your life back on track, your Rules for Living are what will keep pushing you forward on days when you feel like giving up.
- Perseverance is the difference between those who succeed and those who fail. By continuing to do over and over again the things that are pushing you towards success, you will eventually break through to the other side and realise all the hard work was worth it.

CHAPTER 13:
LIFE AFTER 'FIRED'

Go confidently in the direction of your dreams! Live the life you've imagined.

Henry David Thoreau

Since I was fired for the second time, my life has moved to a place that is so much more incredible than the place I started from. Far from being the life-shattering experience I thought it was at the time, being fired twice really has been the best thing that ever happened to me. Once I recognised the covert opportunity and was able to grasp that all the pain and heartache were part of the lesson, I went about rebuilding my life. The lessons I learnt from both times I was fired laid the foundation for a life that was richer, more honest, more rewarding and more fulfilling than it ever had been before.

Ultimately, my experiences of being fired have made me a wiser person. My values have changed and I look at life a little differently to those who have never lost their jobs. I enjoy my work more and ironically, I believe I'm a better employee. In my personal life, I've learnt to hustle and look deeper for opportunities to grow and improve my life.

When I look at life now – post-unemployment – there are five key lessons I learnt that have shaped my new life. Some of the lessons – like the need for multiple income streams – are practical and aim to safeguard me should the future hold similar challenges. Others, like the new perspective I bring to being an employee, are more to do with personal growth and constant learning. But all five lessons were worth the scars I received to learn them. They have made the life I have today so much better than I could ever have imagined.

THE ART OF THE SIDE-HUSTLE

Waking up in August 2014 with a great new job was only the start of the new life I planned to create. I had learnt some hard lessons from unemployment, the biggest one being that no matter how safe and secure you feel, life can change in an instant and you'd better make sure you have another means of survival outside of your job. In this modern age, having a single income stream is the biggest risk you can take. Having multiple income streams is a necessity in our lay-off-prone society.

One of my coaching clients recently introduced me to the word 'side-hustle'. We were discussing the need for multiple income streams, and I was explaining to her the various other vocations I have besides working in my 9-5 job. 'Amazing!' she said ' what a great side-hustle!' I instantly fell in love with the word.

In 2016 everyone should have at least two side-hustles. Ideally they bring in some extra cash but at the very least they give you a sense of purpose in life that extends beyond your day-to-day job. I wish I'd had a side-hustle back in January 2014.

Fast-forward to 2016 and I have three side-hustles. Today I still have a wonderful job working in marketing. I love it; it challenges me and I am happy to walk in there every day. However, unemployment set a fire inside of me that I can't imagine experiencing any other way. The vulnerability of being fired without an ounce of warning made me vow to never again be in a position where the only income I received was from my main job. I wanted to create another dimension to my life – one full of side-hustles – so I could feel the assurance that no matter what happened in my life I was in control.

I am a property investor. Over the last 18 months, I have built up a small, but profitable portfolio of houses that provide a passive income stream which would be enough to live off in the event of being fired again. I now spend my weekends on building sites checking on the renovation of my properties or driving around town viewing new properties to purchase. I love watching a house go through the transformation from a run-down wreck to a modern new home for my tenants.

I am also a coach. Being fired and rebuilding my career provided a solid base for helping others in establishing their goals and achieving their dreams. Of my three side-hustles, this is by far the most rewarding. Getting to spend time with amazingly talented people who are looking to fulfil their potential is like nothing else I have ever done.

And finally, if you are reading this book, I am a published author.

What do you do?

Recently, for the first time in my life, I didn't have an instant answer to the question, 'what do you do?' When asked this question at an event, I paused for a few seconds and replied, 'Well, I'm a property investor, but I'm also a coach. And I'm writing my first book. Oh and I work in marketing. I'm a Property Investor/Coach/Author/Marketeer!' I had become a 'slashie' - that's 'Property Investor' SLASH 'Coach' SLASH 'Writer' SLASH 'Marketeer'.

A 'slashie', for those unfamiliar with the word, is a word used to describe someone who has many vocations. If you live in a city like London, you are bound to know at least one slashie. In my building alone I could name about 25. A girl who is an actress/model/blogger, or a stylist/writer/DJ. Or the guy downstairs who is a director/photographer/waiter. In 2016, slashies rule the world.

Forbes recently wrote an article about slashies (although they are yet to coin the phrase). Their article focused on the art of the side-hustle, acknowledging that technology and an uncertain economy had given rise to the side-hustle, particularly amongst millennials. No longer do we look to climb the corporate ladder and stay in the same job for 30 years; we are comfortable with multiple part-time jobs and calling ourselves a photographer/blogger/life coach.

Whether you have just been fired, or you are happily working in your day-to-day job, it's never a bad time to add a side-hustle. A good side-hustle will give you a sense of purpose over and above getting up every day to go to work. It will make you feel like you are moving somewhere, that you are constantly learning and, if you are really lucky, that you are making a contribution to the world. I only wish back in January 2014 that I'd had at least one side-hustle.

Side-hustles – where to start

If you are struggling to figure out exactly what constitutes a great side-hustle, there are plenty of websites you can consult. Many sites like Business Insider and Mashable have articles about people who side-hustle. The most popular side-hustles are things you can do from the comfort of your own home. Websites like Upwork have become incredibly popular for people who want to side-hustle as editors, copywriters, graphic designers, social media managers. There are also so many part-time jobs you can do on the side. I have a friend who works full-time in marketing but also works part-time as a fitness instructor in some of London's coolest fitness studios.

Alternatively you can start your own business. As crazy as it sounds, there are many businesses that can be run on the side. Network marketing has become very popular in the age of the side-hustle. In a network marketing business you are given the tools and infrastructure to set up your own business, so you have the support to quickly learn the basics of how a business runs, leaving you with time to focus on getting the sales.

For me the utopia is a side hustle that generates passive income; something that you can work on today, but that will keep putting money in your pocket long after the hard work has finished. Property is a great example of this. Once a house is renovated and rented out the money flows in with very minimal additional effort. Writing a book is also a fantastic way to generate passive income. Someone once told me that there is a book in every one of us, and now with the world of self-publishing there is no excuse not to become a published author. If you look, you'll find no end of ideas!

NETWORK, NETWORK, NETWORK

The second lesson being fired taught me is just how precarious our network is if we rely 100% on the people we know inside work. Not only can you suddenly lose your entire support network if you find yourself fired, but you are in danger of missing out on all the other opportunities for connection that exist outside your company walls.

I was definitely guilty of creating a social network that was almost exclusively connected with my workplace, but my stint of unemployment taught me the value of talking to people. Not 'networking' in the traditional sense, but just getting out and meeting new people. This is something I still do today

As so many amazing people had been so generous with their time during my job hunt, as I re-entered the workforce it was important to me to repay the favour. Nowadays I very rarely turn down the opportunity to meet someone new or connect acquaintances. If people introduce me to a new person, it's not unusual that I'll invite them for coffee. Usually there is no specific reason and it is rare that there is something in it for me; I just love to keep in touch with the world outside my job. It's great to meet new people, to hear their story and remember that there is a big exciting world out there where people are doing amazing things.

It takes time but I try to meet at least one new person or an old acquaintance per week. The best meetings are ones where I can then introduce my new acquaintance to someone else in my network – just like people did for me when I was job hunting. I love the idea that I'm connecting up all these fabulously talented people who are going to collaborate and go on to change the world! Whether that actually happens, I have no idea but it's a lovely thought. Regardless of the direct outcome, I always feel uplifted and inspired after a coffee with a new acquaintance, plus my network is growing and new opportunities are always coming my way. I know it is something I never would have taken so seriously had I not been fired.

THE 'FIRED' EMPLOYEE

If side-hustling and networking changed the way I approached life outside my job, the next big lesson I learnt was about the way I approach my day job. I can say without doubt that the experience of being fired has, ironically, made me a much better employee.

When work is your main purpose in life, anything that takes place during the workday carries such a huge importance that it's easy to feel like every issue or grievance at work is of enormous significance. We take it personally when we are passed over for a promotion or we get upset and frustrated when projects don't go our way. And yet for the most part our jobs are only important because we treat them like they are a lifeline. That's why we freak out when we are fired; because someone has cut your imaginary lifeline. But we forget that in reality, it's simply a job.

I know this better than anyone. In my previous life, my work was all-encompassing. It wasn't that I was working 18-hour days all the time - nothing like that, in fact. It's just that the work and the company and the people in the company, meant so much to me. It was hugely important for me to be successful, because my work and the people I worked with were the most important things in my life. My family lived on the other side of the world so it was very easy for work to fill that void. As such, I put a lot of pressure on myself. When things didn't go right I would blame myself and get frustrated and stressed. When things got crazy busy I would let the situation overwhelm me.

'We're not saving lives here...'

When I got too stressed, an old boss used to say to me, 'We aren't saving lives here, we are just selling trainers!' It would always make me laugh and stop to reflect for a moment... before continuing on with my stress! But she was right about one thing: most of us aren't saving lives. We are contributing to the world for sure, and hopefully making a good contribution but lives don't hang in the balance as the result of our work. Yet you wouldn't know it from the way we behave. We place such an all-encompassing importance on the work we do every day, that it's hard to look rationally at life .

There's a reason that women who go on maternity leave with their first child come back to work more calm and chilled-out than before. It's not because maternity is some sort of year-long spa retreat! It's because they come back to work with a new set of priorities. This realisation helps them to remember during times of pressure and stress in their careers, that there are far bigger things in life that could go wrong right now. Having a sense of perspective allows us to make more rational decisions, and ultimately makes us better employees.

Now don't take this as a suggestion that I don't place a huge importance on the work I do. I do - an incredible amount. The difference is that now I don't let things overwhelm me. I don't let the stress of a situation in the office manifest itself into something bigger than it needs to be. I can remind myself that 'we're not saving lives here'. I focus on doing the best work I can but remind myself to keep things in perspective. I'm doing better work because I can keep a calmer, more rational head. Ultimately, I am a much more enjoyable employee to be around. And it's all because I was fired.

PERSONAL LIFE FIRST

The next lesson I learnt from being fired was that I needed to place more of an importance on my personal life. While I am definitely a much better employee as the result of being fired, I also think I'm a much better girlfriend, daughter, sister and friend. I have never been a complete workaholic. I have generally managed to strike a fairly good balance between work and home life but I know there was always a tendency for me to irrationally sway too far towards work. Without consciously acknowledging it I really did believe that we are defined by our contribution to the world through our work

These days things have changed. Being fired really highlights the importance of your family and friends. My seven months of job hunting whilst incredibly tough, were made so much easier by the people who love me. After being fired, it's hard to throw yourself back into work without acknowledging the huge importance these people play in your life. It's crucial to find that balance and go back to work on your terms. Remember, life is what happens when you leave the office. That's where the magic in our lives really happens.

Recently, a close friend of mine was getting married in Bali. The timing of the wedding wasn't great – it coincided with an incredibly important day at work, arguably the most important day of the year. I agonised for months how I would approach this with my boss. My former pre-unemployed self wouldn't have even asked for the time off; I would have rationalised that it would reflect badly on me if I missed this important day. But I am a different person now. I knew how important it was to attend this wedding, not only for my friend, but also for me.

Thankfully, my boss was an absolute superstar. Not only did he give me the time off, his reaction to my requesting the time off was thoughtful and sincere. He got it. He could see how much it meant to me and at no point did he make me feel bad. Five months later, I was in Bali with my closest friends, celebrating the wedding of someone we love.

The happiness that these people bring to my life was highlighted on our third night on the island when my boyfriend and I returned to the hotel after a day at the beach. It was about 11pm and six of my best friends were in the swimming pool with a large bottle of gin. On the edge of the pool they had lined up eight glasses with ice. They all started whooping and cheering as we walked into the villa, demanding we jump straight in the pool. As we swam with our glasses of gin – clearly violating every rule of the hotel – we laughed and cried as we recalled stories from our years of friendship. It was perfect. This is what life is really about.

NEVER REGRET THE EXPERIENCE

My final lesson from being fired was more about personal growth than anything else. After my second stint of unemployment I became somewhat of an expert on the topic amongst people I knew. My experience had been so tough and at times incredibly isolating, that I wanted to be a source of support for other people who were going through the same thing. Every time someone told me about a friend or a colleague who had just lost their job, my heart went out to them. Outwardly I wished for them to immediately recover and get a new job but inwardly I hoped for them that whatever happened, it would build character. While their immediate future may be tough I hope that two years from now they can look back on the experience and be thankful it happened. That was the lesson - never regret the experience. No matter how tough things became, the experience of being fired shaped me and countless others I know in an incredibly positive way.

It's impossible to tell someone who has just been fired that this is the best thing that will ever happen to them. It's not rational - how can having the rug pulled out from under you be good? I certainly don't suggest telling someone you know who has been freshly fired that this is a great situation – it's not. However I hope by writing this book I have managed to dispel some of the stigma of 'being fired'. I want people to feel comfortable with the experience, enjoy the process as much as they can and take the chance to capitalise on the opportunity.

I know what it's like. I have been there. I understand how it feels to think you are a failure; I know what it's like to apply for a job for which you are perfectly qualified but not even get an interview. I remember deeply how it feels to be one of the final two applicants for a role and then miss out just when the end of your unemployment felt moments away. I remember not being able to look the people I love in the eye because I felt like I'd let them down. I really do know how you feel.

The wonderful news that I can share with you is that not one person has ever told me they wished it had never happened. Everyone will acknowledge on different levels how tough it was, but no one ever says they regret it.

Most of the time there was something missing in their lives that being fired helped them see. Once their unemployment ends, they re-enter the workforce a much more balanced person and in most cases much happier. They learn to put themselves and their families first and approach work with a more rational head. They still enjoy their work but their lives are much richer for having been fired.

Being fired is a very real part of modern life. It is by no means the worst thing that can happen to you and it's unlikely to be an experience you regret. It won't feel like it at the time, but hindsight will provide the knowledge that you are better off for having endured it. You'll learn lessons like I did – multiple lessons if you are lucky, and hopefully life-changing ones. But certainly I feel confident that if you seize the day and implement the ideas in this book, regret is not an emotion you will experience when you begin to look back.

KEY LESSONS FROM CHAPTER 13:

- Multiple income streams and networking are two very practical lessons we should all have in place in our lives – whether we have been fired or not!

- Being fired gives you a new perspective on how you approach work and your personal life. This perspective will ultimately make you a better employee but also a better friend and family member.

- If you embrace the opportunity, you will never regret the experience of being fired. It can be the best thing that will ever happen to you.

CHAPTER 14:
THE SUN WILL SHINE AGAIN

It's always darkest before dawn.

My Dad

Recently I was cleaning out my old email inbox and found a beautiful email from my father I received after the first time I was fired. In it he tells me that no matter how bad I feel now, things will get better, that 'it's always darkest before dawn'.

That's the thing about hitting rock bottom. When you finally bounce back up you re-emerge with a sense of invincibility that can never be manufactured. Losing my job and the subsequent months of getting up and working through the mental fog, showed me not only that I could survive, but I could probably have handled much more.

I know when I look back on my life losing my job will not be the greatest crisis I ever face. There will no doubt be great heartaches and loss in my future. There will be health issues, if not for me, I'm sure for someone I love. There may be great financial turmoil and situations that spiral downwards in which I have no control. I'm sure the fog may even return from time to time.

But the so-called failure of losing my job taught me a lot about myself. At 32 years old I thought I knew who I was. It turns out I'd been hiding some pretty powerful character traits underneath my conscious persona. I was way more tenacious than I realised, coupled with an incredible amount of perseverance that I never knew I had. I was able to summon the will to keep going even though I kept getting knocked back for job after job after job.

I also found that I was able to comfort myself in solitude. While it was hard to go it alone, I came to understand I didn't need other people around me constantly to give me strength. In actual fact all the strength and comfort I needed was right inside me and had been all along. This was a very powerful revelation as I am now able to go through life comforted in the knowledge that I can survive on my own.

Conversely, losing my job also helped to highlight the true heroes in my life, people who I already loved who stepped up to another level when supporting me through this tough time. There will never be enough gratitude I can express that would do justice to the people who were alongside me for that seemingly endless time it took to find a new job.

No matter what your experience of losing your job - whether you bounce straight back or end up in a long period of unemployment - choosing to make the experience an opportunity to learn and grow will be the best decision you ever make. There is no denying the experience is difficult. However, if you choose to recognise the wonderful opportunity that has been put in front of you it can become the springboard to huge, previously unimagined success in your life. It's an opportunity to learn, to grow, to try new hobbies and test the water of new careers. You'll find it helps to strengthen your relationships, to build new ones and, of course, show strength in the face of adversity and discover wonderful aspects of your personality that you never knew existed.

After losing my job before Christmas, I found the fog began to lift in the springtime, and by summer my life was back basking in the bright sunshine. My second experience of being fired literally moved with the seasons! Now I wake up everyday and am thankful for having had both experiences. Difficult at the time, they have both nevertheless shaped who I have become and contribute daily to the success I have in my life.

My purpose for writing this book was that I wanted people to feel that they are not alone in this situation. I wanted my readers to feel a sense of connection, to understand that being fired is normal and okay. And that, if you really want it to be, it can be your springboard for success.

By reframing our approach to losing our jobs, we can use the experience to propel our careers and our lives into new levels of success we never thought possible. By focusing on five key areas of our lives, we can start to create the life we really want instead of living the one that comes to us, whatever that may be.

In December 2014, I found myself in Singapore for a week with work. I had only been in my new job and out of the job hunt for four months, so I was still adjusting to my new life - having a steady income, having workmates, having a new structure in my life. It still felt new and exciting to me.

I was very lucky that along with my new job, I had acquired an incredible team of new workmates. In my 12 years of working, I don't think you could have assembled a bunch of people more humble or down-to-earth than my new colleagues. At the end of the week in Singapore, three of my colleagues invited me to go to Bali for the weekend – a two-hour flight and a quick trip to the sunshine before heading back home to London and the cold of December.

As we were only there for two days, we decided to stay in one of the nicest 5-star hotels in Bali. It was over £200 per night – a huge sum of money in Indonesia! We woke the first morning to a beautiful cloudless day and 30-degree heat; it couldn't have been much better.

As we lay by the pool, I was checking my phone to see if I had any messages from home, when I noticed the date. It was the 13th of December, exactly one year to the day since I had been fired.

As I looked across the pool and down to the beach, I felt a sense of calm and happiness that I hadn't felt for a long time. To my left, my workmates were perusing the cocktail list and deciding what beverage we were going to consume; and to my right, the beautiful waves of the Indian Ocean crashed onto Kuta beach. Life could not have been more perfect.

As I lay back in my sun lounger and smiled, the memories of the last year rushed through my mind. It was all still so raw and yet, somehow it didn't hurt anymore. I had learnt the lessons; I had battled my demons; and here I was, in Bali, on the beach, drinking cocktails at 10am with my awesome new friends. That's the thing about life: everything is temporary.

What a difference a year makes. Life was wonderful again.

ACKNOWLEDGEMENTS

This book would not have been possible without the love and support of so many people. Firstly, I would like to thank all of those who encouraged the writing of this book as well as those who supported me with feedback in the final stages of editing – Sandra Grigg, Jay Goddard, Ben Hutchings, Simon Charlesworth, Liz Alder, Karla Chapman and my Mum and Dad.

Special thanks must go to my editor, Meg Ward, whose dedication to editing this book was a huge comfort after many months of writing alone. Thank you for challenging me and pushing this book to be in a better place than where it started.

Huge thanks to my friend Kyle Balmer for his advice and support. Even when we were still relative strangers, you were so helpful and encouraging of this book. Because of you, some people might actually buy it!

The contents of this book would not exist, nor would I have had the confidence to write this, had it not been for the incredible support given to me during both instances of unemployment. For this, I have so many people to thank that a page in a book would simply not be long enough. Both times I was completely humbled by the incredible amount of support I received and for that there will never be enough words to thank everyone. However, I must mention a few key people that were instrumental in getting me back on my feet the second time I was fired; Nicole Hubbard, James Montague and Ben Hutchings (again!), for their support in getting my career back on track; Clive Ormerod, for always believing in my ability and always reminding me to do the same; Amy Thomson and Sandra Grigg (again!) for being the Rocks in my life; and Rebecca Kremsky, who was there by my side the whole seven months, doing the best she could to keep me sane.

Thank you also to the many people whose lives and stories have inspired the contents of this book. Thank you for allowing me to tell your story so that it may in turn enrich someone else's life.

To Brendon, your love and support is felt every day, even when we are separated by thousands of miles of ocean.

And finally, thank you to my family. To my Mum, Dad, Charlie and Sunny. I wake up every day and am comforted in the knowledge that I really do have the best family in the world. Thank you for being so amazing.

ABOUT THE AUTHOR

Stephanie Brown is a property investor, career coach, author and keynote speaker, who continues to maintain a successful career in marketing and communications alongside her other vocations.

Originally from New Zealand, Stephanie now resides in London, United Kingdom. She has worked for over 13 years in marketing for some of the world's most iconic brands, most notably 7 years working in various senior roles for Nike.

Stephanie is passionate about helping other people realise their potential and works with individuals to help them create the life they've always wanted. Her work in coaching and writing is aimed at inspiring people to live every day with gratitude and vitality.

For more information on career coaching and speaking opportunities, please visit www.LifeAfterFired.com

COACHING AND SPEAKING

Stephanie is available for one-to-one personal coaching as well as keynote speaking.

Current career coaching clients include a company director, mid-level advertising agency executive, future company MD as well as clients who have lost their jobs and are looking for the next role.

Stephanie is also available to speak on a variety of topics, most notable in the area of career development and personal growth.

For more information or to book, please visit
www.LifeAfterFired.com

Copyrights and Permissions

Every reasonable effort has been made by the publisher to trace the copyrights holders of material in this book. Any errors or omissions should be notified in writing to the publisher via www.lifeafterfired.com, and we will endeavour to rectify the situation for any reprints or further editions.

Quote by Jim Rohn, America's Foremost Business Philosopher, reprinted with permission from SUCCESS ©2016. As a world-renowned author and success expert, Jim Rohn touched millions of lives during his 46-year career as a motivational speaker and messenger of positive life change. For more information on Jim and his popular personal achievement resources or to subscribe to the weekly Jim Rohn Newsletter, visit www.JimRohn.com or www.SUCCESS.com.

Quote from J.K Rowling Harvard Commencement speech - Very Good Lives – Copyright © J.K. Rowling 2008

Quote from Jean Shinoda Bolen reprinted with permission from Ms Bolen

Quote from Rosabeth Moss Kanter reprinted with permission from Ms Kanter

Quote from Ilya Pozin reprinted with permission from Mr Pozin

Quote from Tim Ferriss reprinted with permission from Mr Ferriss

Quote from Steve Biddulph reprinted with permission from Mr Biddulph

Made in the USA
Columbia, SC
14 June 2021